THE ERA OF THE WITNESS

THE ERA OF THE WITNESS

ANNETTE WIEVIORKA

Translated from the French by Jared Stark

CORNELL UNIVERSITY PRESS

ITHACA AND LONDON

L'ère du témoin, by Annette Wieviorka, copyright © PLON 1998.

Copyright © 2006 by Cornell University

First published 2006 by Cornell University Press
First printing, Cornell Paperbacks, 2006

Printed in the United States of America

Design by Scott Levine

Library of Congress Cataloging-in-Publication Data

Wieviorka, Annette.
  [Ere du témoin. English]
  The era of the witness / Annette Wieviorka ; translated from the French
by Jared Stark.
    p. cm.
Includes bibliographical references and index.
  ISBN-13: 978-0-8014-4331-2 (cloth : alk. paper)
  ISBN-10: 0-8014-4331-8 (cloth : alk. paper)
  ISBN-13: 978-0-8014-7316-6 (pbk.: alk. paper)
  ISBN-10: 0-8014-7316-0 (pbk.: alk. paper)
  1. Holocaust, Jewish (1939–1945)—Historiography.   I. Title.
  D804.348.W5413 2006
  940.53'18072—dc22   2005037538

Cornell University Press strives to use environmentally responsible suppliers and materials to the fullest extent possible in the publishing of its books. Such materials include vegetable-based, low-VOC inks and acid-free papers that are recycled, totally chlorine-free, or partly composed of nonwood fibers. For further information, visit our website at www.cornellpress.cornell.edu.

Cloth printing   10 9 8 7 6 5 4 3 2 1
Paperback printing   10 9 8 7 6 5 4 3 2 1

For Anne-Lise Stern, who has taught me much

CONTENTS

INTRODUCTION

"Good people, do not forget! Tell! Write!" Simon Dubnow is said to have exhorted his companions before he was murdered in Riga by a Latvian soldier on December 8, 1941, during the liquidation of the ghetto.[1] This was the final injunction of an old man who for over half a century had chronicled the history of the Jews. His words may be apocryphal. It is nonetheless true that during and since the destruction of the European Jews, many sought and have sought to tell what happened, as if obeying the imperative to honor what is now called, at least in France, "the duty to remember." Thus, between 1944 and 1948, the members of the Historical Commissions of the Central Committee of Polish Jews gathered 7,300 testimonies, which have since been stored in the archives of the Jewish Historical Institute in Warsaw and which no one to my knowledge has systematically studied.[2]

Moshe Feigenbaum had worked with the Central

Committee of Polish Jews and wanted to emigrate to Palestine. In December 1945, he found himself in Munich, in the heart of the U.S. zone of Germany. This former bookseller born in the village of Biała Podlaska had survived with the help of a Polish farmer by hiding in a makeshift underground bunker in the farmer's orchard. He felt that testimony should be collected not only from the Jews in Poland but also from the tens of thousands of Jewish survivors who were rotting in displaced person (DP) camps in Germany, waiting for a foreign government to admit them. Together with Israel Kaplan, a journalist in Kovno before the war, Feigenbaum created in Munich a new Central Historical Commission alongside the already-existing Central Committee of the Liberated Jews. This commission published a journal in Yiddish, *Fun letstn khurbn* [Out of our most recent catastrophe], and sought to gather testimony systematically. During its three years of existence, it built a network of more than fifty historical committees throughout the DP camps in the U.S. zone. Depositions were taken from more than twenty-five hundred survivors and assembled with over a thousand photographs and other documents saved from the ghettos and the camps. In 1948, this historical commission ceased to exist. Feigenbaum and Kaplan emigrated to Israel, where the collection was deposited in what would become Yad Vashem.[3]

In the late 1950s, Philip Friedman confided to Raul Hilberg that the writings of the survivors had become too numerous to catalog. At last count, he claimed, there were eighteen thousand.[4] That was forty years ago. Philip Friedman (1901–1960), probably the foremost historian of the genocide at that time but whose name and work are totally unknown in France, was already a dedicated historian before the war, which he spent in hiding in his native city of Lvov. From the end of the war until 1946, he directed the historical commission charged, most notably, with collecting testimony in Poland. Afterward, he turned his attention to educational programs for the survivors of the genocide living in displaced person camps in the U.S. zone of Germany. In 1948 he emigrated to the United States and devoted his life to the history of the genocide. This pioneering figure was also the first bibliographer of the genocide, having published three important books: *Guide to Jewish History under Nazi Impact*, *Bibliography of Books in Hebrew on the Jewish Catastrophe and Heroism in Europe*, and *Bibliography of Yiddish Books on the Catastrophe and Heroism*.[5] In all these works, the entries under the rubric "Testimonies" fill many pages.

The number of testimonies was already enormous in the 1950s, and today we are faced with masses of them, perhaps hundreds of thousands, for which no exhaustive bibliography exists. No other historical event, not even World War I—when the practice of recording testimonies first became common—has given rise to such a movement, which is so vast and long-lasting that no researcher can pretend to master it in its entirety. The testimonies that have resulted are of many different kinds, recorded at various distances from the event and in multiple media: there are manuscripts and books, di-

aries, and audio- and videotapes. Some were produced
spontaneously, prompted by a need within the survivor.
Others were delivered in response to requests from various sources related first of all to the demands of justice,
and which led certain survivors to testify in the many
trials that followed the German surrender and that continue to this day in various countries. Other survivors,
in France, Israel, or the United States, have been speaking in schools since the 1980s. Finally, others testify, just
as survivors did in the immediate postwar years, in the
context of large-scale efforts to create oral history
archives, a number of which now exist.

Testimonies, particularly when they are produced as
part of a larger cultural movement, express the discourse or discourses valued by society at the moment the
witnesses tell their stories as much as they render an individual experience. In principle, testimonies demon-
strate that every individual, every life, every experience
of the Holocaust[6] is irreducibly unique. But they dem-
onstrate this uniqueness using the language of the time
in which they are delivered and in response to questions
and expectations motivated by political and ideological
concerns. Consequently, despite their uniqueness, testimonies come to participate in a collective memory—or
collective memories—that vary in their form, function,
and in the implicit or explicit aims they set for themselves.

Whereas testimonies had previously been confined to
archives, their current abundance and ubiquitousness in
the public sphere forces the historian to confront issues
that are at once old and new. They are old in the sense
that historians have always been aware, as Marc Bloch

puts it, that "there are no good witnesses, for no deposition is accurate in all its parts."[7] In principle, historians possess tools forged by their predecessors that enable
them to examine testimonies through a critical historical
lens. With testimony to the Holocaust, however, as with
other "hot" topics of recent history, historians find
themselves in what seems to me an unprecedented situation. Historians do not live in a vacuum. They live in
the same world as everyone else, absorbing the same
newspapers and television programs and concerned with
the same debates, in which they are frequently called on
to participate. Their memories are imprinted with the
same images. Certainly, historians are supposed to be
capable of ascesis, of adopting a critical stance, of holding emotions, likes, and dislikes at arm's length, of sift-
ing through various possible ways of representing the
past, and, when called on to pronounce on issues of
public concern, of saying what is true and just. Yet they
find themselves ceaselessly swept up in the passions of
the day, where problems become entangled and con-
fused, where ethical and scientific concerns at times get
caught up in political issues.

Historians have rarely drawn on the testimonies of
survivors of the genocide and have in fact treated them
with considerable mistrust. Lucy Dawidowicz expresses
an opinion shared by most of her colleagues: "The transcribed testimonies I have examined have been full of
errors in dates, names of participants, and places, and
there are evident misunderstandings of the events themselves. To the unwary researcher, some of the accounts
can be more hazard than help."[8] Thus, for Dawidow-

icz, nothing can be salvaged from testimony, which is seen as incapable of reporting facts in a pure positivist mode and, above all, incapable of generating a historically accurate narrative. Historians have essentially relegated reflection on this gigantic body of sources to literary critics, to the various "psys"—psychiatrists, psychologists, psychoanalysts—and, to a lesser extent, to sociologists. In the study of Holocaust testimony, as in the study of the history of Nazism, French scholars have long been practically absent.

Things move slowly, but they do move.[9] I hope to contribute to this movement by studying the conditions under which testimonies have been produced and how these conditions have changed over time, and by studying the role of testimonies in the construction of history and collective memory. This inquiry is indispensable not only for Holocaust studies. It should also allow us to illuminate processes at work with respect to other historical periods. Just as Auschwitz has come to stand for absolute evil, the memory of the Holocaust has become, for better or for worse, the definitive model for memory construction, the paradigm in efforts to analyze recent events or to create the basis for future historical narratives of events unfolding before our eyes that have not yet become history, for example, those that took place not long ago in Bosnia. Reference to this paradigm may be implicit or explicit. For instance, historians may use the categories and concepts produced in the wake of World War II (crimes against humanity, genocide, and so on) to describe a more remote past, as they have done in the United States with the slave trade and the institution of slavery, or to describe the contemporary era, as in the analysis of communism, which some have said, rightly or wrongly, requires its own "Nuremberg trials." They apply this paradigm to the present whenever they follow the protocols developed over the last half century in relation to Holocaust memory—for instance, when they systematically record victims' testimonies in Bosnia and in Rwanda.

In this book, I seek to understand the various roles and images of the witness and their modification over time by identifying three successive phases. The first phase concerns the testimony left by those who did not survive the events. The second, organized around the Eichmann trial, shows how the witness has emerged as a social figure. The third, finally, examines the evolution of this figure in a society that has given rise to what I call the era of the witness.

I

WITNESSES TO A DROWNING WORLD

"Everyone wrote," observed the historian Emmanuel Ringelblum, "journalists and writers, of course, but also teachers, public men, young people—even children. Most of them kept diaries where the tragic events of the day were reflected through the prism of personal experience. A tremendous amount was written; but the vast majority of the writings was destroyed with the annihilation of Warsaw Jewry."[1] When Ringelblum established an organization in the Warsaw ghetto, which he called "Oneg Shabbat" [Joy of the Sabbath], with the mission of creating a systematic archive of documents concerning the ghetto, he did so in the certain belief—largely justified, by the way—that the contents of the archive would be preserved.

Historians were the first to recognize, in the midst of the genocide, the urgent necessity of bearing witness so that history could one day be written. These historians included Simon Dubnow, Emmanuel Ringelblum, and

Ignacy Schiper,[2] who, before he was killed in Maidanek, confided to Alexander Donat that "everything depends on who transmits our testament to future generations, on who writes the history of this period. What we know about murdered peoples is only what their murderers vaingloriously cared to say about them. Should our murderers be victorious, should *they* write the history of the war, our destruction will be presented as one of the most beautiful pages of world history, and future generations will pay tribute to them as dauntless crusaders. Their every word will be taken for gospel. Or they may wipe out our memory altogether, as if we had never existed, as if there had never been a Polish Jewry, a Ghetto in Warsaw, a Maidanek."[3]

These views were contemporaneous with the speeches of Heinrich Himmler, such as the one delivered before the *Reichsleiter* and the *Gauleiter* in Posen, Germany, on October 6, 1943:

I ask of you that what I tell you in this small circle is only to be listened to and never to be spoken of. We were faced with the question: what about the women and children? I decided to find a clear solution here as well. I did not feel I had the right to exterminate the men—that is, to kill them or have them killed—while allowing their children to grow up and take revenge upon our children and grandchildren. The difficult decision had to be taken of making this nation vanish from the face of the earth. . . . In the countries occupied by us, the Jewish question will be solved by the end of this year. Only remnants of the Jewish population will be left, hidden here and there. . . . Now you know, and you will keep this to yourselves. One may perhaps decide in the distant future to tell the German people more about it. I believe it is better that we—all of us—take this upon ourselves for the sake of our people, that we take upon ourselves the responsibility (the responsibility for a deed, not only for an idea), and that we carry this secret with us to our graves.[4]

The SS would carry this secret to *their* graves because, for Himmler, they were the only possible repositories. From his point of view, the victims posed no threat whatsoever. Although Himmler repeatedly expresses fear of the vengeance of the Jews, which allows him to justify the murder of the children, he never envisions the possibility that the Jews could write the "pages of history." On this point, he was mistaken. Certainly, the desire for vengeance existed among the survivors. At times efforts were even made to act on those desires. Tom Segev describes the revenge planned by Abba Kovner, a major figure in the Vilna ghetto resistance and the man who is said to have written the first tract exhorting the Jews not to let themselves be led like sheep to the slaughter. Arriving in Palestine after the war, this former resistance fighter carried with him an unrealized plan to poison the potable water of several large German cities, hoping in this way to kill six million Germans. And a number of Germans were actually executed. But the poet Hayyim Bialik, as cited by a member of the Knesset during a debate on German-Israeli relations, wrote:

"Not even the devil has devised a fitting revenge for the blood of a small child."[5] The true revenge would be the creation of the state of Israel.

But if vengeance was not the central concern of those who survived, the victims for their part realized quickly—as soon as they took the measure of events—that it was up to them to write this page of history and to unveil to the world what they named with the Yiddish term *Hurbn*, the destruction. Ignacy Schiper states this clearly, even though he was fully aware of the aporia faced by the victims:"But if *we* write the history of this period in blood and tears—and I firmly believe we will—who will believe us? Nobody will *want* to believe us, because our disaster is the disaster of the entire civilized world. . . . We'll have the thankless job of proving to a reluctant world that we are Abel, the murdered brother."[6]

Affirming the unity of the human race ("Abel, the murdered brother" implies the existence of Cain, the German brother and murderer, whereas in Himmler's texts the Jews are expelled entirely from the human race), Schiper displays an extraordinary prescience. The world will not want to know anything about this disaster. Indeed, despite the profusion of testimonies, does the world know? And what does it know? In order to know, one must first nurture the desire to know.

The Nazi project, as articulated in October 1943 by Himmler as it was entering what he saw as its final phase of implementation—it was so perceived by Schiper as well—can be stated simply: to erase a people from the world and from the history of the world. "It has come to pass that the people are losing their children. It is a tremendous loss, of course, and it is anything but easy to console them; but then here comes the *Soïfer* with a loss of his own. . . . For he is among those who are losing their entire people. . . .

"What? . . . What is it that he is losing? . . . But no! A loss such as this is unheard of!"[7]

□ □ □

Realizing he is in the process of losing his people, the *Soïfer*—Yiddish for "scribe," the one who copies the Torah without committing a single error—places his last hope in the written word, without perhaps perceiving an aporia different from the one remarked by Ignacy Schiper. Once a people is dead, once it no longer has a present, how will it write its history? The writing of history cannot take place without "testimonies," in the broad sense that Marc Bloch gives to this term, that is, without traces—of which archives constitute the most basic form—that make that writing possible. Nor can history be written without historians, that is to say, without men and women who, in the present time of their existence and of their experience, of their desire to know, seek to understand and to put this understanding into language in order to communicate it to others, interrogating the past based on the traces that past has bequeathed to them.

The traces left by those who perished in the genocide are hardly lacking. In many places, they were systematically assembled. The most successful of the archives were those of the Warsaw and Łódź ghettos.

The history of the Warsaw ghetto archives is well known. This is due less to their use by scholars—historians have shown little interest in the history of the ghettos[8]—than to a novel that became a best seller in the United States and later in France as well, John Hersey's *The Wall*, which is based on the Oneg Shabbat archives and which models its main character, Noach Levinson, on Emmanuel Ringelblum. By 1939 Ringelblum was already a dedicated historian, but he was also a political activist. He had brilliantly defended his thesis on medieval Warsaw Jewry at the University of Warsaw in 1927 and had taught history in Jewish high schools. While pursuing his research on the Jews of Warsaw, he was simultaneously an active militant in the Zionist movement. In 1930 he began to work part-time for the Joint Distribution Committee (JDC), the large Jewish-American organization created during World War I to aid world Jewry. In November 1938 the JDC sent him on a mission to the Zbazsyn camp, where some six thousand Polish Jews who had been expelled by the Germans at the end of October were interned under extremely precarious conditions. The five weeks he spent there marked him profoundly.[9]

The idea of creating an archive took shape during the first months of the German occupation of Warsaw. Assisted by a small group of friends, Ringelblum began to gather testimonies and reports solicited from among the many Jews who were seeking refuge in Warsaw. He was acutely aware that what was happening was unprecedented. His small group grew, joined by writers, journalists, and activists from across the political spectrum.

It became a veritable resistance organization, one without parallel. They named the group Oneg Shabbat because it met on Saturday, the Jewish Sabbath. The organization collected a wide range of documents: artifacts of cultural life in the ghettos such as posters from theatrical performances or concerts, meal tickets, minutes of meetings of the Judenrat (the Jewish council that administered the ghetto), decrees issued by Nazi authorities, clandestine newspapers, and so on. The archives were divided into three sections, sealed in milk cans or metal boxes, and buried in the ghetto before its "liquidation." After the Warsaw ghetto uprising was crushed in May 1943, the ghetto was systematically razed. Not a single stone of the old Jewish quarter of Warsaw remained. In the minds of the Nazis, not only did the Jews themselves have to disappear, the very environment in which they had lived also had to be eradicated. The ghetto became a desert of stones. To find the buried archives, one had to use "archeological procedures," in the words of Michel Borwicz, who participated in the task.[10] Two sections of the archives were disinterred, in 1946 and 1950, and have been housed since then at the Institute of Jewish History in Warsaw, constituting 60 percent of the collection. They total 1,696 boxes containing approximately 27,000 pages.[11] Some of these documents have been published in Israel, Poland, and the United States, but they are far from being fully utilized.

In Łódź, renamed Litzmannstadt by the Germans, in a region called the Warthegau annexed to the Reich, the ghetto was created very early, beginning in February

1940, and was one of the last ghettos "liquidated," in August 1944. The systematic archiving of documents took place within the Judenrat itself. On November 17, 1940, the leader of the Łódź Jews, Chaim Rumkowski, a highly controversial figure, founded a Department of Archives as in any ordinary administration, the official existence of which was known to the Germans. The Department of Archives constituted the fifth section of the ghetto's department of population records.[12] Nonetheless, certain archives, notably those belonging to the various commissions in charge of ghetto inspections, were kept secret. The principle that motivated the creation of these archives was clearly stated: they were "for future scholars studying the life of a Jewish society in one of its most difficult periods."[13] Josef Klementynowsky wrote a letter to Rumkowski on November 16, 1940, in which he agreed to serve as the archive's first director: "I fully appreciate the far-reaching significance of this treasure house for historians of the future."[14] The archivists received full and complete authority from Rumkowski to collect materials pertaining to all parts of the Jewish administration. Authorization was also given to conduct interviews with representatives of the various agencies and to preserve these in written form, as well as to attend their management meetings. The archives thus include various materials relating both to the German and the Jewish administration of the ghetto: orders, memoranda, speeches, official correspondence, statistical data. But they also include manuscripts and valuable books abandoned by intellectuals who died in the ghetto or were deported. At the same time, the archivists made a first attempt to write the history of the ghetto, undertaking a certain number of monographs. The work was divided into major themes: history of the ghetto, economic problems, religion and culture, Hebrew and Yiddish. According to the historian of the ghetto, Lucjan Dobroszycki, two monographs are particularly interesting because the documents they draw on and cite in extenso date from the first period of the German occupation of Łódź, when the archives did not yet exist. The first of these, written in Polish, deals with the history of the Jews of Łódź from September 1939 to the time the ghetto was hermetically sealed in May 1940. The second concerns the history of Łódź from May 1940 to the end of that year. In addition to these was a sort of dictionary of the Jewish personalities of the ghetto, containing various facts about the administration of the ghetto, and even a lexicological study of words created in the ghetto.

It is from this archive that the chronicle of the Łódź ghetto[15] was born, a project written collectively by a group of people with nothing in common: not age, not education, not country of origin. The initiator was Julian Cukier (1900–1943), originally from an important Łódź family and a journalist before the war under the pseudonym Stanisław Cerski, who worked at the archives and was soon nicknamed "the Plutarch of the ghetto." He surrounded himself with ten to fifteen collaborators. Among them was Szmul Hecht, a native of Wieluń, a town southeast of Łódź. He had been deported to the ghetto during the "resettlement" of the Jews from the provinces of Łódź, Poznań, and Bydgoszcz in the summer of 1942. There was also Dr. Bernard Heilig (1902–1943), a renowned scholar specializing in the economic history of the Jews, on which he had published several volumes. He had been deported from Prague to Łódź in October 1940. Dr. Rosenfeld (1884–1944) was born in Korycany, Moravia, and had graduated from the University of Vienna. He was deported from Prague to Łódź in October 1941. A collaborator of Theodor Herzl, the editor-in-chief of the Zionist weekly in Vienna, *Die neue Welt* [The new world] he had been a correspondent for the major Jewish-British newspaper, the *Jewish Chronicle,* and had translated the classics of Yiddish literature into German. The head of the team was Abram S. Kamieniecki (1874–1943), born in Slonim under the czarist empire when the town belonged to what was called the "Jewish Pale of Settlement," a vast marginal territory stretching from the Baltic to the North Sea where the Jews of the empire were constrained to live. He had received a traditional education, then studied philosophy at Heidelberg, Berlin, and Berne, before specializing in biblical studies.

The men who wrote the chronicle and worked in the archives were employed by the ghetto's Jewish Council. They therefore received supplementary rations like other employees, which did not, however, keep them from suffering cruelly from hunger; some even starved to death. The chroniclers shared the fate of the inhabitants of the Łódź ghetto: death in the ghetto itself or in the deportation, in the death camps of Chelmno or Auschwitz-Birkenau. Only one survived: Bernard Ostrowski, an engineer.

The first bulletin of the chronicle is dated January 12, 1941. The last discovered is that of July 12, 1944. Lucjan Dobroszycki believes that this bulletin is indeed the last. The next day, a Monday, it became clear that the fate of the ghetto was sealed. The 68,561 inhabitants who still resided there were to be transferred to Auschwitz-Birkenau, with the exception of 700 who would stay to clean the ghetto. Between the two dates approximately a thousand daily bulletins were written, each between half a page and ten pages. Lucjan Dobroszycki believes that the number of lost bulletins is minimal, 5 to 10 percent at most. The first section of the chronicle, which runs from January 12, 1941, to September 1, 1942, is written in Polish; the last, from September 1942 to July 30, 1944, is written in German, except that between September and December 1942, German and Polish alternate. Does the difference in language lead to differences in style and content? Lucjan Dobroszycki thinks so. The German of the chronicle, according to him, is laconic, uniform, more lucid, and seems more detached, more distanced than the Polish. Nonetheless, the chronicle is a unified work. Each of its bulletins, regardless of which language it is written in, covers the same subjects—though not every subject appears each day—preceded by headings: the weather in the ghetto; births and deaths, including, in the part written in German, the exact population count given periodically; people killed near the barbed wire surrounding the ghetto; suicides; food supplies and rations; food prices; the black market and various incidents related to contraband goods; public health and diseases; German directives; the various inspection commissions; actions of the ghetto administration; cultural and religious activities; the settlement in the ghetto of Jews from other regions occupied by the Reich; and deportations. There is also one noteworthy rubric, "People Are Saying." Rumors were rampant in the ghettos, and all the testimonies allude to them. Some rumors were knowingly planted by the Germans but others arose spontaneously. The situation in the ghetto, in Łódź as in Warsaw, looked very much like what Marc Bloch describes in his "Reflections of a Historian on the False News of the War": "One can never say to what extent emotion and fatigue destroy all critical sense. . . . Methodical doubt is ordinarily the sign of good mental health. This is why harassed soldiers, with troubled hearts, could not practice it." Bloch also insists on the considerable role of censorship. "By a bold stroke unimagined by even the most daring minds, censorship abolished the work of centuries, sending the soldier on the front back to ancient times and forcing him to rely on means of information and a state of mind predating the newspaper, the printed newssheet, the book."[16] What can be said, then, about the situation in the Łódź ghetto, which was closed in an extraordinarily hermetic fashion? By contrast, the Warsaw ghetto, located in the heart of the city, was always porous. Telephones, for instance, continued to function there until the uprising was crushed in May 1943.

Rumor was so central to the Łódź ghetto that Jurek Becker, a writer who had been in the ghetto as a child and settled in East Germany after the war, placed it at the heart of one of his novels, *Jacob the Liar*. His hero, Jacob, is taken to the police station because he walked through the streets of the ghetto after curfew. There he overhears a radio broadcast by chance. It thrills him. "In a fierce defensive battle our heroically fighting troops have succeeded in halting the Bolshevist attack twelve miles from Bezanika."[17] He aches to divulge this news. But his story—that he left the police station alive—is too improbable to be believed. He therefore pretends that he owns a radio that broadcasts only good news. "It's worth it: hope must not be allowed to fade away, otherwise they won't survive," thinks Becker's hero. "He knows for sure that the Russians are advancing, he has heard it with his own ears, and if there is a God in heaven, they must come at least this far; and if there is no God, they must come at least this far and they must find as many survivors as possible, so it's worth it."[18] In the Łódź ghetto as in the Warsaw ghetto, false news has mainly a reassuring function. It is a trap. It allows the fantasy of a possible liberation and fosters an imaginary connection to a world in which the enemy seeking the death of the Jews is being battled. It counteracts the sense of being excluded from the world, abandoned by all. Marc Bloch recalls that in the last days of the retreat at the beginning of World War I, one of his superiors announced to him that the Russians were bombing Berlin; he did not have "the courage to push away this seductive image; I vaguely felt its absurdity and I certainly would have rejected it if I had been capable of reflecting on it; but it was too pleasant for a depressed spirit in a weary body to muster up the force to reject it."[19] Many of the ghetto chroniclers, their "spirits depressed" and their "bodies weary" from hunger and disease, performed mental operations analogous to the one described by Marc Bloch. This suggests that the study of testimonies could potentially enrich our knowledge of the psychological mechanisms people deploy in extreme situations.

□ □ □

In addition to the ghetto archives, there are diaries, personal chronicles, and stories written by authors hoping to publish them as books. Only some of these have reached us, always by strange paths. A small handful of them has been published, but the Jewish Historical Institute in Warsaw still holds 321 such texts, which were discovered in the ruins, in the garbage dump, and elsewhere, or were given to the institute by survivors or by those who found them by chance. Many also disappeared with their authors. "After each successive deportation," Michel Borwicz relates,

> when the alleys of the ghettos were saturated with a bloody silence and the dwellings were pregnant with the void created by the absence of thousands of people newly torn from their homes, special German units "confiscated" the abandoned furniture and belongings. Debris from the pillaged goods would be left strewn on the sidewalks. Amidst the debris, one could often make out pages covered in writing. Emptied from drawers and from hiding places by the warriors, and judged by them to be without value, they were

thrown outside, consigned to disappearance. This is probably the fate met by the many writings we know existed, sometimes by title or subject, but that have not been found in any preserved collection.[20]

The most celebrated of these chronicles, which was for a long time the only one available in French or English, and even so in an edition whose scientific rigor leaves much to be desired, is the diary Emmanuel Ringelblum wrote in Warsaw in conjunction with his archival enterprise.[21]

Michel Borwicz, who pioneered the study of testimonies but whose work has not received the recognition it deserves, observes that the major wave of ghetto writings and the alterations in their content coincided with a transformation that took place in the collective consciousness in 1942. Until 1942, the belief was "unflagging in Germany's imminent defeat. It thus remained possible and probable that a number of victims would survive the war in safety."[22] After the major deportations from the ghettos to the death camps began, the belief in the imminence of the Nazi defeat did not weaken but was accompanied by a premonition of "the destruction of *the last surviving Jews.*"[23] Borwicz cites a popular saying of the time: "There will be no heir and no memory." Writing thus becomes a vital way to preserve a record of events that defied the imagination and to assure immortality.

The paths by which these writings have come down to us also belong to the history of testimony. Let us take a single example, Simha Guterman's *Livre retrouvé,* edited and studied by Nicole Lapierre. "It is a salvaged book," the sociologist writes in her introduction. She relates that at the end of 1978, two Poles from Łódź, Tadeusz Szczeniak and Josef Pinkert, brought to the Jewish Institute of Warsaw a bottle sealed with wax and containing writings in Hebrew characters. The bottle had been found in Radom during the renovation of a house, hidden under the steps of a staircase. In this bottle were "long and narrow strips of paper, tightly rolled, numbered, and covered in Yiddish writing, so tiny in places as to be almost illegible." Dated from January to May 1942, it was the history of the Jews of Plock, from the start of the German occupation until the "liquidation" of the ghetto.[24]

There have also been documents preserved in archives whose existence was known but whose publication was deferred for practical or ideological reasons. This was notably the case of the diary of the president of the Warsaw ghetto, Adam Czerniakow. In 1968, during a study leave in Jerusalem, Raul Hilberg learned from Josef Kermisz, the archivist of Yad Vashem, that Kermisz possessed Czerniakow's diary, which was written in Polish. How did this diary arrive in Israel? In 1964, the Israeli ambassador to Canada had acquired the journal from a woman named Rosalie Pietkewicz, who claimed she had purchased it in 1959. In fact, under her true name, Rosa Braun, this woman had managed to escape the Warsaw ghetto with Czerniakow's diary and to hide on the "Aryan" side of the city. When she left Poland, she took the diary with her and sold it for ten thousand dollars. It was first published in Polish in the journal of the Jewish Historical Institute of Warsaw, but the critical edition in English, edited by Raul Hilberg and Stanislas Staron, did not appear until 1982.[25] Why was the publication of such a document delayed? Without a doubt, it was because it concerned the director of the Judenrat in the part of Poland with the largest concentration of Jews. Indeed, the question of the role of the Jewish Councils was fiercely debated from the moment of their creation, and their directors were the objects of strong opprobrium. Moreover, those interested in the genocide, who were exclusively Jewish until the 1960s, showed more interest in retracing the history of the Jewish resistance than in analyzing the structures established by the Germans to organize Jewish life in the ghettos and above all to implement their directives. It took some time before publishing such a work became possible. It also took the debates surrounding the Eichmann trial and Hannah Arendt's claims that the Jews, through their councils, had contributed to their own deaths, to get historians to analyze with less emotion the complex situations in which the Jewish leaders found themselves.

The work of Calel Perechodnik, which appeared under the title *Am I a Murderer?* met a similar fate.[26] Calel Perechodnik had been a police officer in the ghetto of Otwock, a small vacation town a few kilometers from Warsaw. He escaped the "liquidation" of the ghetto, during which his wife and two-year-old daughter were deported. After various journeys, he hid in "Aryan" Warsaw and wrote his work there. Perechodnik, like Simha Guterman, died in the Warsaw uprising of August 1944. But he had entrusted his manuscript to a Polish friend, Wladyslaw Blazewski, whom he calls "Magister" in his work. After the war, Blazewski sent the manuscript to Perechodnik's brother, who had spent the war in the Soviet Union. A copy was deposited at the Jewish Historical Institute of Warsaw and remained there, accessible to all, for nearly fifty years. But it was only in 1993 that a Polish historian, Pawel Szapiro, published this singular document—singular because Jewish police from the ghettos have rarely given their testimonies. While a great many people have borne witness, certain categories of survivors have tended to abstain, and still abstain. Primo Levi, for instance, observed that, as concerns the camps, there is no testimony from those who "acquired privilege for themselves by becoming subservient to the camp authority."[27] Nathan Beyrak, who heads one of the major interviewing projects of survivors in Israel, laments the fact that "we haven't managed to interview people who belonged to the Jewish Police, or those who were not particularly nice."[28] Perechodnik takes us into regions where we can go only with great repugnance, to the heart of violence and human cruelty. The psychological acuity and the extreme lucidity verging on cruelty that makes reading this work almost unbearable can probably be attributed to the author's certainty that he will not survive. Ineluctable death authorizes him to reveal feelings and thoughts that he probably would have had to conceal had he been reintegrated into the community of humankind. The certainty of death also allowed him to describe those same feelings in others. How could he have done this if he had envisioned even for a single instant that he would again live among them? We have much to learn from Perechodnik. But then again, we may prefer not to know what certain situations reveal about human nature and social mechanisms.

These writings all have one thing in common: they are writings from beyond the grave. Otherwise, they are quite different from one another. Some are diaries in the proper sense of the term, that is, writings where the authors set down what happens from day to day, what they perceive, what rumors they have heard, how they feel. Others are journals written in a lapidary style. These consist of notes whose essential function is to keep a record of events and facts. For instance, Adam Czerniakow, head of the Warsaw ghetto Judenrat, carried small notebooks with him wherever he went, noting various facts, at times embellishing his notations with a personal reflection or a quotation. As Raul Hilberg explains in Claude Lanzmann's *Shoah,* "Every day, almost every day, he had an entry. He might record the weather, where he went in the morning, and then all the things that had happened. But he never failed to write. That was something that moved him, pushed him, compelled him throughout the years—almost three years—of his life under the Germans."[29] Czerniakow's style is usually, though not always, telegraphic, without literary devices, "a prosaic style."[30] It is an extremely important document. Hilberg "spent about six years with Czerniakow" (187) as "a voyeur, a ghost inside Czerniakow's office" (185), to cite his own words; he observes that Czerniakow's diary forms a bridge between the executioners and the victims.[31] "With him," he writes, "I crossed the boundary, as he went out to hold his difficult official conversations with Germans and as he returned dejected to the Jewish world. I dwelled with him to grasp his struggle with problems of housing, food, starvation, disease, taxes, and police, and to observe him while he had to listen to the incessant wailing of Jewish women beseeching him for help outside his office door."[32] And he concludes, "On the day when the diary was published in the United States, I believed we were opening this vista to a larger public."[33] But Hilberg became somewhat disillusioned. The public did not wish to see what really happened in the ghetto. They did not want to look unless they were given a soft version of events. They did not wish to call into question the basic idea that there was, on one side, the "good," the "heroes," the resistance fighters in the Warsaw ghetto uprising, and on the other side, the "bad," the "collaborators," the members of the Judenrat. Reading Czerniakow entails adopting a state of mind that does not judge. It entails trying to understand a man and the historical role he chose to assume, a role that forced him to face an absolute aporia, until he could bear it no longer and committed suicide. The diary nonetheless found a small readership in its French translation. This is perhaps because Claude Lanzmann filmed Raul Hilberg in *Shoah* discussing his ongoing research on Czerniakow and because he had the historian read passages from the diary for the camera. "At the end," writes Hilberg, "Lanzmann said to me, 'You were Czerniakow.'"[34] It may also be because, as Richard

Marienstras underscores, there is a "strange modernity" in Czerniakow's diary that comes, he claims, "from the way the failed undertakings he describes are obliquely and mysteriously in tune with the aimless world we inhabit, where there can be no success because there is no goal. Everything ends in failure, even when, deceiving ourselves, we think we have reached the conclusion of an effort or a journey or an undertaking."[35] Perhaps it is this "strange modernity" that is so troubling. Czerniakow's diary has not been the subject of any critical studies or rigorous research. We are led to wonder why the two authors most often cited today, and on whom a veritable library is being written, are Primo Levi and Robert Antelme, two survivors of the concentration camp system neither of whom is representative of the Jews killed in the genocide.

We could discuss other diaries from the Warsaw ghettos, written in Yiddish, Hebrew, or Polish, translated into and published in both English and French, such as those of Chaim Kaplan, Abraham Lewin, Mary Berg, or the great schoolteacher Janusz Korczak.[36] One could add to this list the writings that were carefully buried and later discovered around the perimeter of the gas chambers and crematoria of Auschwitz-Birkenau. These writings are of two kinds. First, there were writings by members of the *Sonderkommando,* whose job it was to incinerate the corpses. Of the thirty or so texts we know were hidden in or near the crematoria, only three have reached us: those of Leib Langfus, Zalman Lewental, and Zalman Gradowski.[37] Second, there were writings that people arriving from the ghettos

brought with them in their meager baggage and buried
once they were at Auschwitz-Birkenau.

□ □ □

At times, testimony is transformed into literature. It is
often supposed that history is better transmitted by
works of nonfiction. Above all, at a time when death is
omnipresent, the idea arises that the work of art is eternal, that it alone can guarantee memory, that is, immortality. The trust victims placed in the written word
demonstrates, in the last analysis, their irreducible humanity. In the Łódź ghetto, Abraham Cytryn, an ado-
lescent at the time (he was born in 1927), saw himself
as a writer and bore witness to life in the ghetto in short
stories and poems. Simha Guterman's book—for he
wanted it to be a book and not simply a testimony—is
also a work of literature. "It is clear," writes Nicole
Lapierre, "that it was more than a diary. The author's
literary concerns are evident. He wanted to transform
this chronicle into an actual text—written, deliberately
constructed, divided into chapters, organized around
key scenes and characters. It was to be a book of life,
the ultimate resistance against death and oblivion. He
wrote so that one day, perhaps, in a world in which he
would no longer exist, readers would discover the suffering he and those close to him experienced."[38] *Am I
a Murderer?* by Calel Perechodnik, belongs to the same
category as Simha Guterman's work. After the liquidation of the ghetto of Otwock, when he was hidden in the
"Aryan" section of Warsaw, Perechodnik composed a

veritable book, a paper child, in memory of the two-year-old daughter whom he, as a member of the Jewish police of the ghetto, had himself taken to the *Umschlagplatz,* the boarding area from which the Jews of Otwock were deported:

> Once I wanted to have a child so that I would be remembered after death. Now, when I am completely alone, I cannot leave a creation that lives on after me; I had to beget a dead fetus into which I would breathe life.
>
> These diaries are that fetus—and I believe they will be printed one day so that the whole world will know of Your suffering. I wrote them for Your glory in order to make You immortal, so they will be Your eternal monument. Now, when our daughter no longer lives, this second baby must be nursed and protected until such time when no power can destroy it. . . .
>
> Now I feel an immortality in myself because I have created an immortal work. I have perpetuated You for the ages.[39]

What could be clearer? What fuels this writing is a protest against death, a need to leave a trace and to assure a legacy.

The first testimonies, those of the period of the ghettos and of their annihilation, are the testimonies of people who did not survive. In different ways, they obey a common desire, that of an individual seeking to rejoin the collective. Knowing he is about to die, the witness also knows that he leaves no descendants, that no one will say the prayer for the dead for him or commemorate the anniversary of his death according to Jewish tradition. And he knows as well that the people to which he belongs will be effaced from the earth. What can he do so that memories and history do not vanish altogether?

□ □ □

This first wave of testimonies did not end with the liberation of the European continent from Nazism. It continued in two principal forms. Yiddish poetry occupies a special place here: "Poetry, *considered as testimony,* is the human voice saying that which is irreducibly human," writes Rachel Ertel, who has devoted a seminal work to this topic: *Dans la langue de personne* [In the language of no one].[40] This phase continued in another register through the collective compilation of memorial books, or *Yizker-bikher*.[41] Just after the German surrender, historical committees formed in the displaced person camps and established commissions to collect the testimonies of survivors and to record the chronology of the massacre. But the chronicle of the massacre could not be disassociated from life before the genocide. For the Yiddish world, what took place was the *Hurbn,* the destruction, not because the number of victims was immense but because the entirety of their world had been destroyed. No longer does the professional chronicler—the erudite rabbi or Talmudic scholar, the historian or ethnologist—control the pen. Now everybody has a voice. "Everyone wrote," Ringelblum observed of the Warsaw ghetto. After the liberation from Nazism, those who survived wrote in their turn. To have lived in a Jewish community and to have escaped the genocide, even if one lived out the war in Palestine or in the United States, safe from Nazism, was enough to legitimate writing and speaking. The writings and words of the survivors were assembled in *Yizker-bikher,* which are situated at the intersection of two traditions: one, the memorial tradition of the *Memorbukh,* which contained a community's martyrology; and the other, that of the Jewish historiographical school born after World War I, some of whose major figures I have already mentioned, and which adopted for Jewish history the methods used at the time by historians studying other subjects. In effect, every *Kehila,* every Jewish community, had a *Memorbukh,* in which, for instance, the names of those who died for the *Kiddush Hashem,* the Sanctification of the Name, during the massacres coinciding with the Crusades were recorded. The genocide, which memorial books usually call the *dritter hurbn,* the third destruction, which followed the destruction of the two temples by two thousand years, created a new situation. The massacre no longer means simply the destruction of a particular community or the death of a particular person. It means the total abolition of a collectivity, of a culture, of a way of life, of what is called *yiddishkeit.* Everything that allows individuals to orient themselves— a language, a history, a land, a social network—and that normally provides the framework for memory and memorialization—is effaced. We might meditate on a beautiful text by Richard Marienstras in an effort to comprehend what the genocide meant for those individuals who survived it.

Let a Frenchman try to imagine—but could he imagine this fully?—France erased from the map, and finding himself with a handful of French speakers among people totally ignorant of the collectivity to which he belonged and whose language, manners, landscape, history, cuisine, institutions, religion, and economy now defined the concrete modalities according to which he could belong to the human race. What then would be his sense of life, what possibility would he have to participate in the *project* of the community that welcomes him, except in the most superficial way? Even if the project doesn't seem to him simply derisory or inept, even if he grew—because the animal in man is strong—to imitate all the gestures of those who, around him, were preparing a future in which his own way of life would have no place—how could he give to this project the same devotion, the same commitment as those around him, who, as they were acting, could project the old into the new and, in the creative movement of life, perpetuate themselves while reinventing themselves, reconstructing themselves based on an image that would not radically, absolutely, and intolerably negate that which they are and that which they were?[42]

The compilation of memorial books emerges from the will or the need to remember, to resurrect an annihilated world with printed words. It is a collective work of mourning that seeks, through stories and photographs, to reconstitute the lost object on paper and to retrace its death throes. The significance of this body of writing is therefore evident. It makes possible what I attempted with Itzhok Niborski, that is, a concrete and relevant reflection on how collective memory is constructed, since the four hundred or so published memorial books form a largely homogeneous corpus, an ensemble of narratives and testimonies to lived experience, sometimes idealized, written by a living collective and, in fact, a surviving collective. All societies work despite and against death. But this society exists also for, with, and in death. Its culture—that is, its collective legacy of memories, knowledge, norms, and modes of organization—is meaningful only because older generations die and because this culture must be ceaselessly transmitted to new generations. The survivors of the Holocaust who came from a Yiddish world found themselves with a culture bereft of meaning. The broken bridges behind them prohibited any return, and the transmission of this culture to new generations appeared extremely problematic. Those who compiled the memorial books hoped to rescue the dead from oblivion. As Edgar Morin writes, "The violence of the trauma produced by a denial of individuality implies a no-less-powerful affirmation of individuality, whether one's own or that of a loved one. An individuality that balks at death is an individuality that affirms itself against death."[43] Memorial books, with their processions of portraits and litanies of names, sought a way to save the dead from nothingness. Those who edited these books honored an implicit testament that must be understood in the Hebrew sense of "covenant"—not with God, but a covenant of the living with the dead. The specificity of an individual never exists in isolation. It is the group that confers it. The rediscovery of a singular dimension implies the reconstruction of that collectivity and its culture with the instruments of memory. There again, the individual rejoins the collective.

The memorial books have been neglected, both by their authors and by their authors' descendants. They have not been transmitted, even though transmission was the objective their authors initially assigned to themselves. The generations born after the destruction, after the Shoah, turned a blind eye to the world of their grandparents. As Jews without a heritage—Alain Finkielkraut speaks of the "imaginary Jew"[44]—they felt that Judaism had bequeathed to them only the ashes of the crematoria. The connection between generations had been broken by the death of the grandparents, or more prosaically, when the grandparents had survived, by the fact that they could not communicate: the grandparents spoke French poorly, the grandchildren did not know Yiddish. Memorial books insist on an indissoluble link that is supposed to connect the generations born after World War II to the memories of Jewish life "before" the genocide. However, this much-desired link, so often invoked, proved impossible. Something had been ruptured that made it impossible to for younger Jews to orient themselves in relation to a collective history. The generations born after the war did not even dare conceive of a story retracing their origins [*un roman d'origines*]. Recollection and commemoration seemed impossible. The void opened by the genocide always tripped them up. The memorial books were thus cemeteries that no one ever visited. When Itzhok Niborski and I published *Les livres du souvenir: Mémoriaux juifs de Pologne* in the early 1980s, at a time when memory and the quest for origins were constantly being invoked, we hoped to call attention to what we judged to be an exceptional corpus. But nothing came of it.

The memorial books exhibit their debt to the *Memorbikher,* most notably by including lists of names of the dead. Serge Klarsfeld's work, whether intentionally or not, also belongs to this tradition. The publication of the *Memorial of the Deportation of the Jews of France,* produced from the lists of deportees categorized by convoy, produced considerable shock. Families whose dead had no graves at last knew the fate of their relatives. The special bond that was formed between Serge Klarsfeld and a portion of French Jews is most likely due to the *Memorial.* With the publication of the *Memorial of the Children,* Klarsfeld sought to restore an identity and a face to each of the eleven thousand children deported from France and murdered in the gas chambers of Auschwitz-Birkenau—not only to restore life but also to capture its final moment. Klarsfeld's work is a form of testimony and of testament, even if the texts he exhumes, notably children's letters, strike a very different tone from ghetto writings. What makes these letters poignant is less what they say than the ultimate fate of their authors. Whereas the ghetto writings present us with a society confronted by cruelty, violence, and death, threatened with the reality of the destruction, the children's letters force us to confront young lives full of promise before they were hunted down systematically in every corner of France and in other European countries, sent to the swamps of Upper Silesia, and put to death for no apparent reason.

Reading the names of the dead has become a fundamental feature of public and national rituals of commemoration. Until the end of the 1980s, however, the
names were read only in cemeteries on a selected day
during the period called the "fearful days," between
Rosh Hashanah, the Jewish New Year, and Yom Kippur,
the day of repentance. These commemorative ceremonies were therefore semiprivate, performed beside
tombs created by community groups or political organizations, tombs that were really cenotaphs, since engraved on them were the names of those without graves,
"victims of Nazi barbarism." Such ceremonies have not
disappeared, but attendance has steadily dwindled. At
certain tombs, such as those belonging to the Bundist organization Arbeter Ring, the names of the dead have
been engraved only in Yiddish, a language that the second generation of immigrants is generally unable to
read.

The names are no longer read only in cemeteries but
also in public places. The readings are no longer addressed only to specific communities—religious or community groups, veterans of a political movement—but
to all, to the descendants of the victims as well as to
Jews from the Mediterranean who did not experience
the Nazi occupation, and even to non-Jews. In a law
adopted on April 21, 1951, the Knesset designated 27
Nissan, the fourth month of the Hebrew calendar, as
Yom Hashoah, the day of commemoration of the genocide. Every year on this day, men, women, and children
congregate in Jerusalem, and at the site of the Vélodrome d'hiver [winter velodrome, a cycling stadium] in

Paris, and at the Capitol in Washington D.C., to read and hear the litany of names for twenty-four hours straight.

Memorial books raise the problem of the language of testimony, a problem that gnawed at the Yiddish-language poet Abraham Sutzkever[45] when he was approached by the Soviets and asked to testify at the Nuremberg trials, at which he was the sole witness to the annihilation of the Jews. In the diary he was keeping at the time, he wrote on February 17, 1946: "I will go to Nuremberg. . . . I feel the crushing responsibility that I bear on this journey. I pray that the vanished souls of the martyrs will manifest themselves through my words. I want to speak in Yiddish, any other language is out of the question. I spoke about this with Ehrenbourg, prosecutor Smirnov, and all the others. I wish to speak in the language of the people whom the accused attempted to exterminate. I wish to speak our *mameloshn* [mother tongue]. May it ring out and may Alfred Rosenberg crumble. May my language triumph at Nuremberg as a symbol of perdurance."[46] Arriving in Nuremberg on February 21, 1946, Sutzkever wrote in his diary: "And I, perhaps the only surviving Yiddish poet from all of occupied Europe, came to the Nuremberg trial not merely to be deposed, but as a living witness to the immortality of my people." The next day, the poet noted that Rudenko, the Soviet prosecutor, had already advised the U.S. prosecutor Jackson of Sutzkever's desire to testify in Yiddish. The only obstacle was technical. "This will be the first deposition of the trial in Yiddish. I pray to God they find a translator." In the following days, Sutzkever learned that the Soviet prosecutors had procrastinated and that the number of witnesses they were allowed was being reduced proportionally. "The odds that I will be able to testify," he wrote on February 25, with the Soviet case set to conclude the next day, "are becoming increasingly slim." And he added, "I sense that there are some reservations about my appearance on the witness stand." Finally, he did testify, on February 27, 1946, for thirty-eight minutes—in Russian.

The question of the language of testimony is, then, fundamental. It is not only a question of knowing in which language a particular witness best expresses himself, or how the choice of language affects the witness's ability to plumb the depths of memory, as we would be led to believe by the discussions that preoccupy the many organizations devoted to the systematic collection of testimonies, all of which are influenced by psychoanalysis to varying degrees. Instead, the question of language is at the heart of a double question crucial for the historian: where does one testify from, and what does one testify to? Does the witness testify to the existence and nature of the world of the Nazi concentration camps? With extraordinary acuity and each with their particular talents, this is the case for Charlotte Delbo, David Rousset, Robert Antelme, and, for Primo Levi, who focuses on the nature of the camps even though he is Jewish. Or does the witness testify to the death of a people? Xavier Léon-Dufour, analyzing the uses of the word "witness" in the New Testament, observes: "The ultimate testimony was that of blood, which the two witnesses [in Revelation] poured out after they had prophesied. In English we even refer to a witness by the same Greek designation 'martyr'; a witness is associated with the destiny of the one to whom he witnesses."[47] As Rachel Ertel writes, Yiddish is

> the only language that shared its fate with its speakers. Even though it survived here and there, with some individuals or some marginal groups, it died at Auschwitz, Maidanek, Treblinka, and Sobibor with the people that spoke it. Yiddish writers and poets are thus the only ones who speak from the depths of the death of their people, and from the depths of the death of their language. They are the only ones to write in a world of deafness, with the consciousness of being without a family lineage, the only ones to write in no one's language. The death of a language is irremediable. If the Yiddish literature of the Disappearance is not comparable to any other, as Elie Wiesel says, it is not because it is more authentic, but because it speaks from within a double death.[48]

It was in Yiddish that Elie Wiesel wrote his first book, his first testimony, *Un di Velt hot geshvign* [And the world was silent], ten years after he was liberated from Buchenwald. A very different version of this book would be published as *La nuit* [Night].[49]

Wiesel wrote the Yiddish version of the book very quickly in 1954, while he was crossing the Atlantic in an ocean liner traveling from Europe to Brazil. The book was published in Argentina in 1956 by Mark Turkow. It was the 117th volume in a series that enjoyed great success in the Yiddish world, *Dos poylishe Yid-ntum* [The Jews of Poland], despite the fact that Wiesel came not from Poland but from Transylvania, a region that was at times part of Hungary, at times part of Romania. Only one other work from this important series has been translated into French, belatedly: the Warsaw ghetto memoirs of the actor Jonas Turkow, *C'était ainsi . . .* , written immediately after the war based on documents the author hid in the Warsaw ghetto and later retrieved.[50]

Un di Velt hot geshvign runs 245 pages and is significantly longer than the French version, *La nuit* (178 pages). In French, Elie Wiesel's work was treated as an ordinary literary work. By 1958, the publisher of *La nuit,* Éditions de Minuit, had already published several accounts of survivors of concentration camps, such as François Wetterwald's *Les morts inutiles* (1946), and in 1960 would begin publishing the books of Charlotte Delbo. But even so, *La nuit,* unlike the Yiddish version, was not part of a specialized collection aimed at a limited audience.

A U.S. historian, Naomi Seidman, has undertaken a meticulous comparison of Wiesel's two works. The difference in the length of the two accounts can be attributed primarily to the fact that the Yiddish version is attentive to details, while the French version is more elliptical. To give just one example: *La nuit* presents Sighet, Wiesel's native town, as "that little town in Transylvania where I spent my childhood."[51] In *Un di Velt hot geshvign,* Sighet is not a "little town" but "the

most important city [*shtot*] and the one with the largest
Jewish population in the province of Marmarosh."[52]
Wiesel then gives the history of the town. Whereas the
dedication in the French version reads: "In memory of
my parents and of my little sister, Tsipora,"[53] the Yiddish version is dedicated "to the eternal memory of my
mother, Sarah, my father, Shlomo, and my little sister
Tsipora—who were killed by German murderers." In
the United States, where Wiesel is the embodiment
of the survivor, Seidman's article provoked violent polemics reminiscent of those seen in France in the spring
and summer of 1997 in response to the testimony of Lu-
cie and Raymond Aubrac. This was because Seidman
claimed that between the two works the figure of the
survivor undergoes a transformation, that the survivor
in the French account is not the same as that in the Yiddish version. And the difference is not simply one of details, it is fundamental.

In *La nuit,* as in *Un di Velt hot geshvign,* the narrator seems to deplore the fact that in the days following
the liberation the survivors were obsessed solely by the
quest for food and that they did not seek vengeance:

> Our first act as free men was to throw ourselves
> onto the provisions. We thought only of that. Not of
> revenge, not of our families. Nothing but bread.
> And even when we were no longer hungry, there
> was still no one who thought of revenge. On the fol-
> lowing day, some of the young men went to Weimer
> to get some potatoes and clothes—and to sleep with
> girls. But of revenge, not a sign.[54]

The Yiddish version, though it contains the same episode, attributes a different state of mind to the younger survivors. Although they are also not bent on vengeance, they display toward the Germans—who are named as such, which they are not in the French version—violence, cruelty, and a desire to humiliate the newly vanquished. For instance, in the Yiddish version the girls are not slept with, they are raped.

Most significantly, the two epilogues, of *La nuit* and of *Un di Velt hot geshvign,* convey different meanings and call for close examination. In *Un di Velt hot geshvign,* Wiesel writes:

> Three days after liberation I became very ill; food-poisoning. They took me to the hospital and the doctors said that I was gone.
>
> For two weeks I lay in the hospital between life and death. My situation grew worse from day to day.
>
> One fine day I got up—with the last of my energy—and went over to the mirror that was hanging on the wall.
>
> I wanted to see myself. I had not seen myself since the ghetto.[55]
>
> I looked at myself in the mirror. A skeleton stared back at me.
>
> Nothing but skin and bones.
>
> It was the image of myself after death. It was at that instant that the will to live awakened within me.
>
> Without knowing why, I raised my fist and shattered the glass, along with the image it held. I lost consciousness.
>
> After I got better, I stayed in bed for several days,

jotting down notes for the work that you, dear reader, now hold in your hands.

But . . .

. . . Today, ten years after Buchenwald, I realize that the world forgets. Germany is a sovereign state. The German army has been reborn. Ilse Koch, the sadist of Buchenwald, is a happy wife and mother. War criminals stroll in the streets of Hamburg and Munich. The past has been erased, buried.

Germans and anti-Semites tell the world that the story of six million Jewish victims is but a myth, and the world, in its naïveté, will believe it, if not today, then tomorrow or the next day.

So it occurred to me that it might be useful to publish in book form these notes taken down in Buchenwald.

I am not so naïve as to believe that this work will change the course of history or shake the conscience of humanity.

Books no longer command the power they once did.

Those who yesterday held their tongues will keep their silence tomorrow.

That is why, ten years after Buchenwald, I ask myself the question, Was I right to break that mirror?[56]

The ending of *La nuit* is infinitely more condensed, and the broken mirror acquires a fuller symbolic meaning:

One day I was able to get up, after gathering all my strength. I wanted to see myself in the mirror hanging on the opposite wall. I had not seen myself since the ghetto.

From the depths of the mirror, a corpse gazed back at me.

The look in his eyes, as they stared into mine, has never left me.[57]

The factual elements are identical in the two accounts: sickness, the onset of healing, the broken mirror. Elie Wiesel gives two different versions of the same episode. What differs is the way the two accounts interpret and explain these factual elements, which, when all is said and done, is what really matters. As Antoine Prost notes, "To say that a narrative is explanatory is a pleonasm. One can separate a narrative from the documentation on which it is based and from the proofs it advances, but unlike a list of facts, even one in chronological order, a narrative cannot be separated from the explanatory links it establishes between the events that constitute that narrative. To tell is to explain."[58] In *Un di Velt hot geshvign,* the Jewish survivor shatters the image of death. This act can be interpreted, as the narrative itself suggests, as a sign of rebirth. He wants to live, he writes, he is fighting so that the world will remember, so that the Nazi criminals, as a popular refrain of the time put it, would not be allowed to walk free in the streets, so that Germany, whose army had been rebuilt according to Wiesel, would not be able to repeat what it had done. Writing is at once an act of revenge and a means of combating something that was not yet called negationism. There is nothing original in Wiesel's position. He is one of a cohort of witnesses who, along with the organized groups of survivors of the deportation and of the genocide, together affirmed, ten years after the liberation of the camps, the necessary battle against forgetting and who placed this battle within a framework that must be understood as political, since it condemned the Germany of the time and the danger it represented.

In *La nuit,* by contrast, the survivor is both living and dead, a split personality who, as he continues on his path, is accompanied by his dead double as by a shadow.

Naomi Seidman sees the existence of these two versions as the manifestation of a conscious desire, a calculated strategy on Wiesel's part. Wiesel wants to play to two audiences, addressing himself in turn to the Jewish and non-Jewish worlds, adapting his discourse to the different expectations of each audience. As concerns the non-Jewish world, the style of *La nuit* appears in this light as a way of seducing his first reader, the man who sponsored the project, prefaced the book, and so legitimized Wiesel as a writer, namely, the Catholic author François Mauriac. It is *La nuit*—the second, reworked version, and therefore, it is implied, a less "true" version than the first—that has "attained mythical status," Naomi Seidman observes with some surprise.[59] She attributes this success to the preface Mauriac contributed to the 1958 edition and that accompanied every subsequent French edition of the text as well as many of its translations. To her, the image of the survivor that emerges from *La nuit* is shaped by Mauriac: "a Lazarus risen from the dead, yet still a prisoner within the grim confines where he had strayed, stumbling among the shameful graves."[60] And it is precisely this image that Wiesel deliberately shattered in the epilogue of the Yiddish version of his book.

□ □ □

Silence in all its dimensions—existential, theological, literary—is one of the major themes of reflection for U.S. and Israeli scholars of the Holocaust and its literature. *La nuit* stands as the paradigmatic example of this theme. The abundant commentaries on *La nuit* consequently revolve around the mystery of God's silence in the face of evil, the muteness of death, and the impossibility of accounting for the genocide in language. These events are said to be unnameable, unrepresentable, unsayable.[61] To quote again from *La nuit:* "Never shall I forget that nocturnal silence which deprived me, for all eternity, of the desire to live. Never shall I forget those moments which murdered my God and my soul and turned my dreams to dust. Never shall I forget these things, even if I am condemned to live as long as God Himself. Never."[62] But Wiesel did not invent these themes. They were already hammered out in the testimonies written in the ghettos as well in the accounts that appeared in French in the immediate postwar period, in those that focused on the Nazi concentration camps and in those that focused on the genocide.[63] For reasons related both to the moment when Wiesel published *La nuit* (1958), when the memory of the genocide was beginning slowly to emerge, and to the incontestably literary dimension of the text, which Wiesel revised with the guidance of the remarkable editor Jérôme Lindon,[64] Wiesel's book has become the quintessential expression of the theme of silence. For Naomi Seidman, it therefore establishes the foundations of a new theology inaugurated by a new covenant, according to which the death of God (or his absence, his silence) is compensated for, as it were, by the birth of the eternal memory of the witness. "Auschwitz is as important as Sinai," Wiesel has declared.[65] In the Jewish tradition, the gift of the Torah to Moses seals the Covenant. All Israel is present at Sinai: Moses's companions, of course, but also past and future generations. It is an ahistorical vision, if such a thing exists, because it abolishes the essential attribute of history, directional time. But though religion mocks history, the historian cannot laugh at religion. Historians must understand its discourse and evaluate it on its own specific terms. This does not mean of course that historians need believe in the discourse they analyze, nor that they seek to transfer religious criteria to their own historical narratives. In fact, when historians analyze literary texts in a critical fashion, they must keep in mind that they are not dealing with archival documents. When they engage with writers, they must keep in mind that writers are unlike the historian, that they are in quest not of a factual, positive reality but rather of a literary "truth" of another sort. They must also keep in mind that writers write using literary conventions, even as they are ready to subvert these conventions. Writers write from within literature, with literature as the point of departure.

Elie Wiesel was educated in the Jewish, more specifically Hassidic, tradition, and in Yiddish literature. The theme of the breaking of the covenant concluded at Sinai is a recurrent theme in the "Yiddish literature of the Catastrophe," as specialists in Yiddish literature have demonstrated.[66] Let us take a single example, which I borrow from Rachel Ertel, a poem by the great Jewish Soviet writer Peretz Markish, "The Mound." It was inspired by the Ukrainian pogroms of 1919, which, in the context of the civil war that followed the Bolshevik revolution, resulted in the murder of tens of thousands of Jews and changed the scale of the massacres. Deaths in the pogroms before World War I were counted one by one, with the largest massacres killing dozens. Later, victims began to number in the thousands and tens of thousands. World War I marked the beginning of mass murder, in the Jewish world and in the rest of Europe. Peretz Markish's poem, whose title refers to the piling up of cadavers—the "heap"—"becomes a litany of blasphemies, invectives, and anathemas against men and against God and culminates in the termination of the Covenant":

O Mount Sinai, lick the blue sludge in the sky's inverted
    scales
And groan, groan like a cat at midnight prayers.
The heap-king spits the ten commandments back in your
    face.[67]

Naomi Seidman thinks that in *La nuit* Wiesel strikes a compromise between an authentic Jewish writing and the expectations of non-Jewish readers, first and foremost François Mauriac. The price of this compromise is, in the first place, a renunciation of the desire for vengeance. We have seen, however, that this renunciation was something largely shared by the survivors. More important, martyrs in general and Jewish martyrs in particular have come to be identified with a renunciation of vengeance. According to Seidman, however, Wiesel concluded a sort of bargain with Mauriac: Mauriac gives Wiesel his moral guarantee, the power of his literary stature, finds him a publisher, prefaces his book. Even more, he dedicates his *Life of Jesus* "to Elie Wiesel, who was a crucified Jewish child." In exchange, Mauriac is empowered to give birth, as it were, to Wiesel the writer, by allowing him to find a language capable of holding the attention of both Jews and Christians.

Seidman's article provoked a powerful emotional response and violent debate in the United States, understandably so, since, beyond her interesting and relevant observations, Seidman quite simply accuses Wiesel of lying. She points out what she considers "compromises." Wiesel forgets to mention, for instance, that the first version of his text was composed at Buchenwald, immediately after the liberation. This "compromise" can only be strategic, aimed at hiding intentions that the historian must unmask. In this sense, Seidman belongs to that category of historians who track down the ways testimony changes, how it deviates from "the truth," without ever seeking to understand the role of testimony in the psychological evolution of the witness and of the collective conscience. Anyone familiar with the conditions under which the first testimonies were produced, immediately after the witnesses were liberated and when many survivors were prone to a "hemorrhaging of expression," in Robert Antelme's words, will find the phenomenon of writing a first testimony and later forgetting it confoundingly commonplace. When those first words were poured onto paper, there was probably no thought of writing a book, there was simply the compulsion to be free of certain elements of one's experience and to reclaim, through these scribblings, one's own identity. On a much smaller scale, the process is analogous to the one that possessed "the man with the splintered world" for twenty-seven years, as described by the psychologist Alexandre Luria. This man, the victim in 1943 of a head wound that caused permanent brain damage, sought, through writing, to "recover his past in order to have a future." "He wrote because it was his only connection with life, his only way of not capitulating before his illness, and of emerging from it."[68] One would be justified in thinking that the function of the notes Wiesel and so many others poured onto paper immediately after the liberation, and whose existence they often forgot, had an identical function: the reconstitution of identity.[69]

In analyzing alterations in testimony simply by comparing Elie Wiesel's two books, pointing out what she considers "compromises" in *La nuit*, Naomi Seidman calls into question the very basis of the literature of testimony. She does so without taking into account the nature of these two texts or the conditions under which they were written. But as Philippe Lejeune has amply demonstrated in his work on autobiography, a narrative is never a raw slice of life. It is always a "literary" text that obeys certain conventions. Above all, Naomi Seidman does not perceive the extraordinary paradox that arises from the two "epilogues." The Yiddish version was published in 1956, when the Yiddish language was in its death throes, when its readers lived isolated in societies that had been spared by the Nazi occupation or had given refuge to the survivors. This readership had over the years been steadily dwindling. Viewed in this light, the Yiddish epilogue is wholly optimistic. It signals the rebirth of a combative Wiesel. The French epilogue, by contrast, is absolutely pessimistic. Does not Wiesel pay for his entry into French literature with the death of his own language, a language in which he will no longer write his books, but to which he will remain nonetheless bound?

To this man, who pioneered the teaching of the literature of the Shoah in the United States, Yiddish remains the language of the witness par excellence. "It is perhaps necessary to emphasize," he writes, "that there is no language like Yiddish for remembering the dead. Without Yiddish, the literature of the Destruction would be without a soul. I know that we write in other languages, but no comparison is possible. The most authentic works about the Destruction, in prose and poetry, are in Yiddish. Is it because the majority of the victims were born into and lived in this language? Let the experts answer that question.

"As for me, I know one thing: if my first book had not been in Yiddish, if I had not written my memoirs in Yiddish, my other books would have sunk into muteness."[70] Wiesel's first book thus had a cathartic function, as Rachel Ertel underscores: "It gave him back his voice, but a different voice.

"For this, he had to traverse death twice: he is a survivor of physical death, and a survivor of the death of the language."[71]

Wiesel's ability to write about that world in French, the fact that he was among the very few who could transmit the stories of this world, probably explains the role he assumed as the herald of memory, in the United States more than anywhere else. The texts he taught and the allusions he makes in his novels are all borrowed from the vanished Yiddish world. By successfully converting this world into a non-Jewish language, he was able to attain what every writer seeks: readers. Wiesel—and in this he can be compared only to Primo Levi—sees himself as both a surviving witness and as a writer. The lament that runs through his memoirs on the gap between his personal fame and the sales figures for his books is a writer's lament. He received the Nobel Peace Prize but not the prize in literature. Whether he is a good or bad writer is not for me to judge. Primo Levi suffers from the same desire to be recognized not simply as a survivor but as a true writer. In 1979, by which time he had published a number of works whose themes and form were quite distant from testimony (*The Monkey's Wrench, The Periodic Table*), Levi still had not achieved the status to which he aspired. "In 1979 nobody in the literary world was interested in Primo Levi," wrote a young critic. "I was the first to consider him as a writer rather than as a witness and chronicler of the *Lager*. It grieved him not to have obtained that recognition."[72]

□ □ □

Incontestably, the survivors of the Yiddish world carry with them the memory of the Shoah. For a time, the Yiddish world may have harbored the illusion that, despite its eradication from Eastern Europe where it had flourished since the Middle Ages, it would be reborn elsewhere, in France, in Argentina, or later in Israel. Nevertheless, a consciousness of loss and a desire for memory were immediate, contemporary with the events themselves. The survivors' rare efforts to make the world confront the genocide, however, were bound to fail. The example of the New York memorial, the first stone of which was laid in 1947 but which was never built, is representative of these failures.[73]

On Riverside Drive between 83rd and 84th Streets in New York City, on the banks of the Hudson, a passerby can see a plaque surrounded by a small iron fence and bearing the inscription: "This is the site for the American memorial to the heroes of the Warsaw Ghetto battle April–May 1943 and to the six million Jews of Europe martyred in the cause of human liberty."[74] On October 19, 1947, a crowd gathered for the unveiling of this plaque, which was supposed to serve as the first stone of the first memorial in the United States, and even in the world. A box containing soil from the concentration camps and a proclamation written by the Chief

Rabbi of Palestine were also sealed in the plaque. The text of the plaque reflects the times, in the United States and elsewhere. The six million dead in the Shoah are placed in the shadow of the glorious heroes of the Warsaw ghetto uprising, which becomes, on the model of Stalingrad, a "battle." They died for the cause of freedom.[75]

This memorial was initiated by a single man, Adolphe R. Lerner, a Polish Jew who fled Vienna in 1938 and reached the United States after passing through France. During the war, he worked for a Polish press agency noteworthy for its efforts gathering information on the annihilation of Jews who had participated in the Resistance. After the war, he presided over an organization of Polish Jews in New York and decided that the Jewish victims should have a memorial. He established a committee, obtained a site from the mayor of New York, and found a sculptor, Jo Davidson, and an architect, Eli Jacques Kahn. In January 1947, the committee began to raise funds for the monument. In November 1948, models of the proposed memorial were exhibited at the Jewish Museum in New York. The model showed a realistic monument representing various figures deemed emblematic: a hero, a religious supplicant of the Jewish faith, a man aiding a wounded person, and a dead body lying on the ground, all placed atop eight steps. But the committee did not like the sculpture. A competition was then organized and an exhibition of models was held, first, at the Jewish Museum, and then at the Museum of Modern Art. A different design, by the architect Erich Mendelsohn and the modernist sculptor Ivan Mestrovic, was approved by the committee and by the New York City Art Commission. The only thing lacking was money. But the committee was unable to raise what was needed. In fact, it did not garner any strong support at all. At the end of the 1940s and the beginning of the 1950s, Jewish organizations had other political and financial priorities: support of the state of Israel, assistance to survivors in displaced person camps in the U.S.-occupied zone in Germany and to those who were beginning to arrive in the United States. According to Rochelle Saidel, such organizations were also afraid of displeasing Germany, since the German Zionist Nahum Goldman was in the process of negotiating what would be called "reparations" with Konrad Adenauer. They also feared that in the Cold War and McCarthyist period an anti-Nazi project might be considered procommunist. A memorial could draw attention to the fact that many of the Jewish resistance fighters were communists. Furthermore, the survivors, who were also new immigrants, were treated like second-class citizens. At the time, interest in the genocide of the Jews, in the United States and elsewhere, was extremely limited. Besides *The Diary of Anne Frank,* which was published in 1952 and made into a film in 1959, and a play based on the memoirs of Gerda Weisman Klein, which was on Broadway at the same time, there were few Holocaust-related publications. The difficulties Raul Hilberg faced in publishing his thesis are well known.[76] Elie Wiesel had trouble finding a publisher for *Night,* the English translation of *La nuit,* which did not appear until 1960. In 1954 this first memorial project was abandoned. As Rochelle G. Saidel writes: "In retrospect, it is more remarkable that an effort at memorialization was initiated . . . than that it failed."[77]

One might object that in France, as early as 1951, someone was fighting to erect a memorial, that he too faced considerable obstacles, and that he was not supported by the major French Jewish organizations. But Isaac Schneersohn succeeded where Adolphe Lerner failed.[78] This was because he did not start from scratch. In 1943 he had founded the Center for the Documentation of Contemporary Jewry (Centre de Documentation Juive Contemporaine, or CDJC) in Grenoble, when that city was under Italian occupation. After the liberation of the French territory, and thanks to men such as Leon Poliakov, the CDJC was able to collect considerable documentation. It supplied materials to the French prosecution at the Nuremberg trials and earned the gratitude of men such as René Cassin and Edgar Faure. During the 1940s, it published a number of works that are still authoritative. Schneersohn was the first to understand that the written word was not sufficient to assure the continuity of memory. Struck by the example of the Tomb of the Unknown Soldier at the Arc de Triomphe and by the cult of the dead of World War I it had engendered, he perceived that memory is better served by rituals than by chronicles, and set out to erect a memorial in Paris to those who had died in the Holocaust. In 1953, the first stone was laid, angering the Israelis who, denied the privilege of being the first to initiate such a project, immediately voted into law the creation of Yad Vashem. In 1956 the memorial was inaugurated. Until the early 1960s, it was the only public memorial located in a public space in the world.

In Jewish neighborhoods, survivors had erected memorial cemeteries—cenotaphs, really, because engraved on them are the names of the victims, which are read aloud each year. In a strict sense, these cenotaphs foster a memory that is collective because it is the memory of a group, though a small one. But this collective memory was closed to the outside. Very little of it, if anything at all, seeped out into the broader social world and spread. Indeed, this memory was ignored or rejected by those outside the Yiddish world. There was no social demand for this memory or this history. The biography of Jacob Shatzky illuminates this phenomenon.

Shatzky, "the historian of the Warsaw Jews," as he is commonly called, belonged to a new generation of Jewish historians, several of whom I have already mentioned, educated in Polish and German universities and who studied the history of Judaism. Born in Warsaw in 1893, a soldier in the Polish Legion of Pilsudski in World War I, he was part of the official Polish delegation to the Conference of Versailles. In 1922 he defended his thesis, *The Jewish Question in Poland during the Period of the Paskiewicz (1831–1861),* then left Poland for New York where, in 1925, he founded the U.S. branch of the Yidisher Vinshaftleher Institut [Jewish Scientific Institute], or YIVO.[79] He was conducting various research projects there when word arrived of the uprising in the Warsaw ghetto and its liquidation. YIVO entrusted him with the task of writing the history of the

Jews of Warsaw. Between 1947 and 1953, Shatzky published three volumes of his *Geshikhte fun Yidn in Varshe* [History of the Jews of Warsaw]. It is a gigantic and unique work that, sadly, covers only the period before 1897 because Shatzky had to stop work on it. Several documents show the despair caused by his acute awareness of the decline of secular Jewish culture based in Yiddish. In 1947 he wrote his wife a letter from Brazil, where he was attending a conference: "The Jews are far from Yiddish culture and in general from matters cultural. One is either for Palestine or the Soviets. The dream of a Yiddish culture in America is falling apart and I see clearly how my life has gone for nothing."[80] He is radically pessimistic even about the possibility of conducting research on the Jewish communities of Poland. He explained himself at the 29th annual conference of YIVO in 1955: "What and how should the Jewish history of the former communities in Europe be researched[?] Detailed research falls to the wayside. Political and economic history also fall aside. They are not part of the inheritance which can be transplanted wherever Jews live. Only intellectual history remains, the history of Jewish culture in the broadest sense of the word."[81] Above all, the writing of the third volume of this history exhausted him, and he laments: "For whom am I slaving? For whom am I writing and about whom? My people is dead, my theme is a dead one and I am dead-tired."[82] The years 1954 and 1955 were a time of intense depression for Shatzky. He died in 1956 of a heart attack and never completed the fourth volume of his history of the Jews of Warsaw, the one covering his own lifetime.[83]

Shatzky poses a double problem. First, there is the difficulty of writing about a vanished world, one that, in the case of the Jews of Warsaw, itself suffered a double disappearance: that of the Jewish people of Poland and that of the environment in which they lived. The meaning of this double disappearance must be assessed. Literature may do this better than a historical account. Abel, one of the characters in a story by the novelist Adolf Rudnicki, returns to Warsaw from a prison camp where he spent the war.

> But when Abel passed Krasiński Square and reached the area of the former Jewish district he looked to the left and to the right, before and behind him, and though accustomed to other parts of this most devastated town in the world, he could not believe his eyes. Expecting devastation, he had expected traces which would make it possible to re-create what had once been here. There were no traces. There were no houses more or less burned, more or less destroyed—there were simply no houses at all. . . . Rubble now lay where a city had once stood. . . . There was a nothingness of an obliterated city, whose ephemeral, indistinct and delusive form loomed in the mind of the spectator.[84]

The Jews of Warsaw and Jewish Warsaw have both disappeared. One could roughly extend this remark to all the Jewish populations of central and western Europe, those of Poland, of the Ukraine, of the Baltic states, of Russia, and so on.

The second problem posed by Shatzky is how to

write the history of a world that has vanished when it is no longer possible to maintain a minimal continuity between life as it had been and the life of the historian. All history is contemporary. It interrogates the past from the point of view of the present. When the present no longer exists, what questions can the historian ask of the past? "There are no more Jews in the world. This nation does not exist. It will never exist again," declares Marek Edelman, the only survivor of the officers' corps of the Warsaw ghetto uprising.[85] He is not speaking of the Jewish people as a whole, of course, but of the Yiddish-speaking segment that was destroyed by the "Final Solution."

□ □ □

In the period immediately following the Holocaust, the survivors did not emerge as a coherent group in any part of society—not even in Jewish communities themselves—in the United States, in France, or in Israel. The Jewish survivor associations that had been created were based on simple ties of sociality and mutual aid and did not harbor ambitions to address anyone except those who had lived through the same experience. The rare efforts they made to bring memory to public attention were largely in vain. In this respect, Paris was the exception. The Tomb of the Unknown Jewish Martyr, which spurred many debates and incited the Knesset to adopt the law creating Yad Vashem, was inaugurated in 1956. For a long time, it would remain the only memorial.

Personal, individual memories, confined within closed, family-like groups, had been generated from the moment the events took place. But these memories were not part of the cultural mainstream and had little political meaning. Before the memory of the *Hurbn* could penetrate the public sphere, the political climate would have to change. Testimony would have to become relevant beyond its personal meanings. Its importance would have to be recognized by society. This would take place with the Eichmann trial, but the price would be alterations in the content and the meaning of this memory.

II

THE ADVENT OF THE WITNESS

The Eichmann trial marks a pivotal moment in the history of the memory of the genocide, in France and the United States as well as in Israel. It opens a new era, in which the memory of the genocide becomes central to the way many define Jewish identity, even as the Holocaust demands to be admitted to the public sphere. Scholars from various countries who have studied the evolution of the construction of memory have all noticed this shift.[1] The trial itself was also powerfully innovative. Everything happened there for the first time. For the first time, a trial explicitly set out to provide a lesson in history. For the first time, the Holocaust was linked to the themes of pedagogy and transmission, themes with a promising future since they are now present in many countries and in various forms: in the inclusion of the Holocaust in school curricula, in the creation of memorial museums aimed at the young, and in the establishment of video archives, one of whose aims is the production of multimedia pedagogical materials. Whereas excerpts of the Nuremberg trials, filmed in their entirety, were shown on newsreels, images from the Eichmann trial, also filmed in its entirety, were broadcast internationally on television. For the first time as well, a historian, Salo Baron, then a professor at Columbia University, was called to the witness stand to provide a historical framework for the trial, and not a single question was raised about the relevance of a historian's testimony. But most significantly, and of primary interest to me, the Eichmann trial marks what I have called the advent of the witness.

A brief consideration of the context in which the trial took place is necessary here. On May 23, 1960, the Israeli prime minister Ben-Gurion informed the Knesset that "a short time ago the security services apprehended one of the most infamous Nazi criminals, Adolf Eichmann, who was responsible, together with the Nazi leadership, for what they called 'the final solution to the Jewish question'—in other words, the extermination of six million of Europe's Jews. Adolf Eichmann is already imprisoned in this country, and will soon be brought to trial in Israel under the Nazi and Nazi Collaborators (Punishment) Law of 1950."[2] The decision to abduct Eichmann and put him on trial was fundamentally political. Several motivations intersected and overlapped. For Ben-Gurion, it was a matter of "recalling to worldwide public opinion whose followers are those who are planning the destruction of Israel, and whose accomplices they are, consciously or not."[3] It was perhaps also a matter of exalting the heroism of the Israelis, in contrast to the supposed passivity of their ancestors; of shaming the world for having abandoned the Jews; and of inducing the major powers to lend more support to the state of Israel. The trial may also have been motivated by a desire to reduce the schisms that threatened the cohesion of the young Jewish state. Abba Eban, then Israeli minister of education and culture, makes this perfectly clear in his memoirs:

> There was a gap between the new urban middle class and the old rural elite based on the kibbutz movement. There was a gap between both of these and the struggling disinherited proletariat in the slum areas and shanty towns. There was a gap between the European-educated population and their sabra offspring and the oriental immigrants. . . . There was also a generation gap: the young Israeli generation born in the sun and under the open skies was given to a simpler, less tormented, but more superficial intellectual outlook than that which had been common to the pioneering generation. There was a gap of alienation between young matter-of-fact Israelis and the more sentimental, complicated, introspective but creative Diaspora Jews.[4]

But Abba Eban also remarks that "there were certain common memories which often reminded Israelis that history had dealt with the whole of the Jewish people in a special way, so that in the last resort they were indivisible in their fate. One of the moments of unifying truth came with the capture and trial of Adolf Eichmann."[5]

The trial, then, obeyed both Israel's domestic and

international political imperatives. It is clear that the genocide was, to use a now-common expression, instrumentalized for political ends. But this instrumentalization was only possible because the attitude toward the Jews had been changing slowly but tangibly since World War II. All signs pointed toward this change.

By the early 1950s, the fate of the refugees from the Holocaust ceased to be the political problem it had been. The last DP camps where Jews had sat rotting, waiting for a country to welcome them, had been closed, and their occupants had been able to emigrate, mainly to the United States and Israel.[6] On September 27, 1951, the chancellor of the Federal Republic of Germany made the historic declaration in the Bundestag that "unspeakable crimes have been committed in the name of the German people, calling for moral and material indemnity, both with regard to the individual harm done to the Jews and with regard to the Jewish property for which no legitimate individual claimants still exist. In this area, the first steps have been taken. Very much remains to be done. The Federal Republic will see to it that reparation legislation is soon enacted and justly carried out. Part of the identifiable Jewish property has been restored; further restitution will follow."[7] The question of German "reparations" preoccupied Israel and the diaspora for months, until an agreement was signed between Germany and Israel on September 10, 1952. The "reparations" disbursed to Jewish organizations of the diaspora, to the state of Israel, and to survivors, under the auspices of the Conference on Jewish Material Claims against Germany, allowed, at least in western Europe, a sort of material normalization in the lives of most of the survivors, who by that time had chosen their country of residence. Against the background of the Cold War, political debates, whether concerning the fate of Jewish displaced persons, as in the United States, or "German reparations," as in Israel and in countries with strong Jewish communities, unfolded at a time when, paradoxically, memory in the sense we understand it today had reached a low point. The publication of testimonies and the placement of commemorative plaques, frequent in the three years following the German surrender, had ceased.[8]

At the end of the 1950s, however, interest in the genocide seemed to be growing. A number of important books were published in France: Elie Wiesel's *Night* in 1958; *The Last of the Just* by André Schwarz-Bart, which won the Goncourt Prize in 1959; and Anna Langfus's *The Lost Shore,* which won the Goncourt in 1961. The publication of testimonies by Jewish and non-Jewish survivors of the Nazi concentration camps also resumed. The decisive factor in this could have been, banally enough, the passage of time, which in a certain way allows lived experience to be metabolized and transformed into literature. It is striking to note that the rate at which survivor narratives were published parallels that of the testimonies to World War I from 1914 to 1948, which Antoine Prost has studied. From 1915 to 1922, Prost observed, there was a first wave of narratives and novels. After that, there was "not silence, because some books were still being published, but at least a clear slowdown in the rate of publication. Publishers thought the public was tired of war stories."[9] Things changed in 1927–1928, some ten years after the end of the war, as they did in 1958–1959 with regard to the testimonies of the victims of Nazism. It was in 1928 that the translation of Erich Maria Remarque's novel *All Quiet on the Western Front* enjoyed its enormous success, signaling in general a "second wave of war books."[10] Time had done its work. "Memories settle, become less troubling, the wounds heal. It then becomes possible to exchange impressions and stories. It is a way of verifying one's own memories, of confirming for oneself the authenticity of an experience too burdensome not to be shared now."[11]

German judicial procedures also resumed, even before the abduction of Eichmann. The German surrender had been marked by a wave of trials unlike that following any other war. No one can forget the trials of major war criminals that took place in Nuremberg from November 1945 to October 1946. But the definition of "major" is too often forgotten; in the context of the Nuremberg trials, it meant those who had been responsible for crimes in more than one country—in other words, the political officials of Nazi Germany. The other criminals, those who had committed their crimes in one country only, had to be judged in the country in question. Judicial procedures varied from nation to nation. Certain criminals were tried in ordinary civil courts, for example, in Norway, Denmark, and Yugoslavia, and others by military tribunals, in Czechoslovakia and Poland, for instance. Depending on the country, criminals were judged by ordinary penal codes, by special laws pertaining to the Nazi period and applied retro-actively, or by a hybrid system that adapted existing legislation. Thus, to take a single example, Rudolf Höss, the commandant of Auschwitz, was taken to Poland, tried in Krakow, and sentenced to death and hanged at Auschwitz. In other countries, notably France, different judicial procedures were used to deal with French citizens tried for treason as opposed to Germans such as Klaus Barbie—sentenced to death in absentia in 1952 and 1954—or Karl Oberg and Helmut Knochen, who were both tried in 1954, sentenced to death, and finally pardoned by the president of France. In Germany, trials also took place in each of the occupied zones, leading to the indictment of 5,006 persons, of whom 794 were sentenced to death and 486 eventually executed. This class of trials included the twelve trials conducted by Telford Taylor at Nuremberg called the "successor trials" or the "trials of professionals," in which doctors, lawyers, businessmen, members of the *Einsatzgruppen,* and others were tried. At the same time, trials began before German courts, with Germans judging Germans for crimes committed against other Germans. The number convicted—5,288, most for minor crimes—remained low, however. Evidence was difficult to gather and the suspects could often not be located. In effect, "most Germans were so concerned with immediate worries about food and housing that they had little time for what they considered politics, and investigating Nazi crimes appeared to most as a political, not a legal or a moral matter. The military government trials and the denazification effort also appeared to many Germans as examples of victors' justice, of political activity by one side against another, defeated side. As a result, they became cynical about the whole idea of punishing people for what they did under Hitler."[12]

In 1949, with the creation of the Federal Republic of Germany (FRG) and the German Democratic Republic (GDR), military governors were replaced by Allied high commissioners who ceased to exercise juridical power and remanded Nazi crimes to the German courts to be judged by German law. Between 1950 and 1955, 628 new suspects, for the most part former concentration camp guards, were condemned. This is an extremely modest number. The judicial system and public opinion recoiled at recalling the Nazi past. In addition, a new law was introduced in Germany in 1955. Those suspected of crimes punishable by sentences of less than ten years would not be tried; only those suspected of premeditated murder could still be prosecuted. Ten years after the German surrender, when the occupation of Germany (with the exception of Berlin) was over, it was legitimate to think that the past was the past, that Nazism was a closed chapter, that no one, in Germany or elsewhere, wanted to hear about it any more.

In fact, this was only an illusion. The end of the 1950s, in Germany as elsewhere, marked the resuscitation of the memory of Nazism and the resumption of judicial prosecutions.

In 1958, the Central Office for the Investigation of National Socialist Crimes was created in Ludwigsburg, Germany, near Stuttgart. Erwin Schüle, its first director, had led the investigation that resulted in the Ulm trial. An SS commandant responsible for the massacre of Jews of Lithuania in 1941 had been declared not guilty by a denazification court. In 1956, this man, who as a civilian had been a police officer in the city of Memel, demanded to be reinstated to his former position in the police, a position so important that his demand drew the attention of the local press. The affair had considerable repercussions in Germany. At issue were no longer simply crimes committed by Germans against other Germans (or German Jews) or the Nazi concentration camp system, as in the immediate postwar judicial proceedings. This trial concerned instead the first massacres of Jews, those committed in eastern Europe on the heels of Operation Barbarossa in the summer of 1941. The scandal exposed the impunity that the perpetrators of these massacres enjoyed. In the majority of cases, no one ever thought to locate the perpetrators of these massacres. In order to compensate for this injustice, which was no longer considered tolerable, the justice ministries of the *Länder* established a research agency charged with a difficult task, since these crimes had been committed in countries that at the time were located behind the Iron Curtain. The Central Office for the Investigation of National Socialist Crimes therefore created specialized teams that examined each geographical region where massacres had taken place. Information gathered in the inquiry was then transmitted to the tribunal of whichever *Land* had jurisdiction over the suspects. The courts then began to bring actions against the suspects. It was this agency that unearthed the case of the 101st Battalion of Reserves of the German Police, sent to Poland in June 1942, where they committed massacres. The investigation and prosecution conducted by the Office of the Prosecutor of the State of Hamburg took ten years, stretching from 1962 to 1972. The U.S. historian Christopher Browning studied the depositions of 210 of the 500 men who composed the unit. As he himself remarks, his *Ordinary Men: Reserve Police Battalion 101 and the Final Solution in Poland* relies on practically a single source, the judicial interrogations of the accused.[13] Using this same case, Daniel Goldhagen revisited the history of the men belonging to this battalion.

It is in this German context that Eichmann's arrest is situated. What led up to it? Several explanations have circulated. The version of events proposed by Tom Segev seems the most convincing, though it cannot be confirmed by archival sources with absolute certainty.[14] Fritz Bauer, a German Jew who had survived Nazism, was a member of the Social Democratic party and general prosecutor for the state of Hesse. In September 1957, he asked to meet with Israel's representative in Bonn, Eliezer Shinar, and informed him that Eichmann was living in Buenos Aires. He communicated this information to the Israelis because he feared that his own government would reject a demand for Eichmann's extradition or would warn Eichmann. Isser Harel, then the head of the Mossad, the secret service of the Israeli army, sent one of his men to the German prosecutor to verify the information. But Israeli agents were not able to locate Eichmann, probably because not enough energy was devoted to the effort. Two years later, Bauer spoke again with the Mossad: Eichmann had been found and his assumed name was known. If Israel did not act, Bauer would be in contact with his own government, which would demand Eichmann's extradition. Israel acted. Eichmann was kidnapped, drugged, and taken clandestinely to Israel to be judged there in a trial that had multiple ambitions but which was aimed, above all, at providing Israelis and the world with a history lesson.

□   □   □

How could this "history lesson" be delivered effectively? What should be its content? As Hannah Arendt has shown, the Eichmann trial was certainly a show trial in which everything was planned. Just as the U.S. prosecutor Robert Jackson, who answered only to President Truman, was the principal organizer of the Nuremberg trials, Gideon Hausner, who embraced Ben-Gurion's views, was the principal organizer of the trial in Jerusalem.

In his memoirs, published in 1966, Hausner explains at length his conception of the trial. "In any criminal proceedings," he writes, "the proof of guilt and the imposition of a penalty, though all-important, are not the exclusive objects. Every trial also has a correctional and educational aspect. It attracts people's attention, tells a story and conveys a moral."[15] To tell this story, to draw a lesson from it, Hausner decided to place testimonies center stage. The Nuremberg trials served for him as a counterexample. At Nuremberg, the U.S. prosecutor

Jackson had based the case on reams of documents, which many journalists found tedious.[16] "Orders, memoranda, official reports, projects, personal notes, and even the transcripts of telephone conversations intercepted by the Gestapo! It seems that all the official public archives, private or secret, of the Third Reich were conserved by conscientious bureaucrats only to be used afterward against the old rulers of Germany," remarked Didier Lazard, an attentive observer of the trials.[17] There were very few witnesses, either for the defense (61) or for the prosecution (33), even though the trial lasted ten months. Their testimonies, moreover, were unspectacular and little reported in the press, with the exception, in France, of the testimony of Marie-Claude Vaillant-Couturier, who had been deported to Auschwitz on January 24, 1943, in the only transport of female resistance fighters sent there. The witnesses had not been called on to tell their stories, to move the judges or the public present at the trial, but essentially to confirm, comment on, and supplement the content of written documents. The Nuremberg trials marked the triumph of the written over the oral. Hausner, for his part, certainly recognized the merits of documentation. The excellent dossier prepared for him by the police, who were responsible for the investigation under Israeli law, was built entirely on Nazi documents, most of which had been used in Nuremberg. "There is an obvious advantage in written proof; whatever it has to convey is there in black on white," Hausner remarks. "There is no need to depend on the retentive memory of a witness, especially many years after the event. Nor can a document be browbeaten or broken down in cross-examination. It speaks in a steady voice; it may not cry out, but neither can it be silenced." Although at Nuremberg justice was delivered efficiently, that trial, with "a few witnesses and films of concentration camp horrors, interspersed with piles of documents . . . failed to reach the hearts of men." For Hausner, it was not simply a matter of obtaining a verdict. A small fraction of the archives would have sufficed to "get Eichmann sentenced ten times over." He hoped for something more than a verdict: "a living record of a gigantic human and national disaster, though it could never be more than a feeble record of the real events." Hausner consequently decided to base the case on "two main pillars instead of one: both documents and oral evidence." One of the aims of the Nuremberg trials was to prove that Nazi Germany had conspired to conquer Europe. It set out to show the array of crimes that accompanied the war of aggression, so that the perpetrators could be punished and so that there would never be another world war. It saw itself as a historic trial in a double sense: it sought to contribute to the historical record, and it sought to outlaw war. Regarding Eichmann, Hausner had "much more . . . than a desire for a complete record." The trial was addressed to the present time, to the nation's youth. "It was imperative for the stability of our youth that they should learn the full truth of what happened," Hausner goes on to explain, "for only through knowledge could understanding and reconciliation with the past be achieved. Our younger generation, absorbed as it was in the building and guarding of a new state, had far too little insight into events which ought to be a pivotal point in its education."[18] This is an odd remark. It was not because the young were otherwise occupied that they were unfamiliar with the events of World War II. Instead, it was the fault of the leaders of the new state, who believed that neither the diaspora nor the genocide offered any lessons. The Israeli was a "new Jew" whose mentality ought to break radically with the submissive mentality ascribed to those who, as it was then often said in Israel, "let themselves be led like sheep to the slaughter."

Once the objective had been decided, the means to achieve it had to be found. The testimonies of the witnesses were these means. "It was mainly through the testimony of witnesses that the events could be reproduced in court, and thus conveyed to the people of Israel and to the world at large, in such a way that men would not recoil from the narrative as from scalding steam, and so that it would not remain the fantastic, unbelievable apparition that emerges from Nazi documents." These testimonies were not to be written down and read on the witness stand but rather uttered aloud by men and women of flesh and blood. "The only way to concretize it," according to Hausner, "was to call surviving witnesses, as many as the framework of the trial would allow, and to ask each of them to tell a tiny fragment of what he had seen and experienced. The story of a particular set of events, told by a single witness, is still tangible enough to be visualized. Put together, the various narratives of different people about diverse experiences would be concrete enough to be apprehended. In this way I hope to superimpose on a phantom a dimension of reality."[19]

What Hausner says here merits consideration. Thirty years later, Geoffrey Hartman, a professor of comparative literature at Yale and in 1982 one of the founders of the Fortunoff Video Archive, whose mission is to record the experiences of those who survived the genocide, used the same terms as Gideon Hausner in explaining the goals of a project that comprises some three thousand testimonies. Like Hausner, he does not discount the importance of archives: "Without the vast paper trail, of course, generated by perpetrators whose triumphalism was at once punctilious and absolute—without this mountain of evidence assembled and interpreted by academic historians, we would not be able to construct an adequate picture."[20] But for Hartman, the testimonies convey precisely what an analytic historical narrative cannot convey, since "the immediacy of these first-person accounts burns through the 'cold-storage of history.'"[21] Hartman turns to the same image of something immediate and living; he expresses the same desire to appeal to emotion as opposed to the supposedly "cold" character of history written from archival documents.

Gideon Hausner therefore embarked on a search for witnesses because he hoped to reconstitute the various stages of the extermination by moving from one testimony to another. "Above all, I wanted people who would tell what they had seen with their own eyes and what they had experienced on their own bodies."[22]

Hausner reveals how, with the help of the police inspector Michel Goldmann, himself a survivor, he chose the witnesses, reading hundreds of declarations collected by the oral testimony department of Yad Vashem. That department was directed by a former member of the Warsaw ghetto uprising, Rachel Auerbach,[23] who herself had participated in the retrieval of the Ringelblum archives from the Warsaw ghetto ruins. Contrary to a long-accepted notion, the witnesses did not testify for the first time at the Eichmann trial. They were chosen based on their first testimonies, which existed in written form, some published and some transcribed from oral testimony. After an initial screening, Hausner interviewed witnesses to decide who would have the honor of testifying at the trial in front of hundreds of journalists from around the world. It was a veritable casting call. Some witnesses were nevertheless reluctant.

The reluctance to testify was partly due to a deliberate attempt to forget events that in any case came back often enough to plague them in their dreams; they did not want to recall them. But there was also a deeper reason: they were afraid they would not be believed. . . . [When the survivors] finally emerged from the forests, the camps and the hideouts, they felt a great urge to tell their stories. But when they started to pour out their hearts, and told tales so staggering that they were beyond comprehension, a listener would occasionally express some doubt, in word or gesture. More often than not this doubt existed only in the imagination of the narrator, but for many of these deeply wounded and sensitive people this was enough to make them take refuge in silence. They buried their dreadful knowledge deep in their hearts and never brought it up again.[24]

The analysis Hausner proposes here confirms what the survivors themselves had stated just after the war and would restate in the 1980s when pressed to testify. Thus Simone Veil: "It is often said that the former inmates wanted to forget and preferred not to speak. Doubtless this is true for some, but inexact for most. If I take my own case, I was always inclined to speak, to testify. But no one wanted to hear us. . . . It is true that the stupidity of certain questions, the doubts sometimes expressed about the veracity of our stories, or, to the contrary, the 'gourmand' interrogation by those who wanted stories even more horrible than reality to satisfy a sadistic imagination hungry for the sensational incited us to prudence and to choose our interlocutors."[25] According to the U.S. sociologist William Helmreich, "Most immigrants quickly learned not to talk about the war, often rationalizing their reluctance by saying that the stories were too horrible to be believed. Americans frequently responded to such stories with accounts of how they too had undergone privation during the war, mostly food rationing. Moritz Felberman [a survivor] was told by his aunt: 'If you want to have friends here in America, don't keep talking about your experiences. Nobody's interested and if you tell them, they're going to hear it once and then the next time they'll be afraid to come see you. Don't ever speak about it.'"[26] More than 350,000 survivors of the genocide lived in Israel in 1949—one out of three Israelis was a survivor. Nonetheless, in Israel too a sort of consensus was established, summed up by Tom Segev: "The less everybody talked about the Holocaust, the better. Thus the great silence was born."[27]

But it would be wrong to conclude that the reluctance to bear witness, due in part to the difficulties many had in making their experience heard in the immediate aftermath of the war, was shared by all at the time of the Eichmann trial. On the contrary, a crowd of willing witnesses materialized, insisting that they be deposed. This troubled Hausner, who was cautious in approaching them, "apprehending that they were overanxious to get the publicity attendant on their appearance at the trial."[28] What can be said about the publicity that television now provides in our society of the spectacle, publicity that can lead certain witnesses or participants in this history, as in any other history, to go beyond the limits of their testimony, to mold it to conform to what they imagine the public wants, in order to secure a glory that they may not realize is at once ephemeral and fungible?

□ □ □

Hausner's choice of witnesses obeyed a double imperative, historical and sociological. "I wanted to tell what had happened in every area under the Nazis, and I wanted the story told by a broad cross-section of the people—professors, housewives, artisans, writers, farmers, merchants, doctors, officials and laborers. That is why we called such a mixed collection of individuals to the witness box. They came from all walks of life, just as the catastrophe struck the whole nation."[29]

There was still the question of how to prevent errors from slipping into the testimonies "by people who were now being called to relate events of sixteen to twenty years before." To counter this difficulty, Hausner chose to "call those who had given statements at Yad Vashem long ago, or who had put their reminiscences on record in published or unpublished works, since their memories could more easily be refreshed by their writings."[30] But in truth, memory is not "refreshed" by notes, as Hausner thinks. It is the already-told story that becomes memory itself, as Primo Levi observes: "After forty years, I remember most of these things through what I have written, my writings are like a form of artificial memory."[31] Or again Louise Alcan, in her second written testimony: "At the end of June, I wrote down what I remembered. Today what I recall is in fact the memory of my memory."[32]

□   □   □

It was on April 28, seventeen days after the beginning of the trial, that "the court heard the first murmurs of the voiceless dead,"[33] in the person of Ada Lichtman, the first witness from Poland. Prior to her testimony, victims of the period before the Final Solution, of the first persecution of the German Jews that followed Hitler's rise to power, had already been called. Sindel Grynszpan, whose son Herschl had assassinated Ernst von Rath, the third secretary of the German embassy in

Paris, in an act that served as the pretext for Kristall-
nacht on November 10 and 11, 1938, described the extremely brutal expulsion of twelve thousand Polish Jews
from Germany, which had instigated his son's action.
"Those unable to walk were dragged on the road—
blood was flowing on all sides. The bundles we had in
our hands were torn away from us and thrown aside.
They acted most barbarically; that was the first time I
saw the barbarity of the German people."[34] Then, "as
in a relay race,"[35] Benno Cohn took over. He had been
president of the Zionist organization in Germany. He
described the years 1933–1939 in Germany, before his
emigration to Palestine, while others described the An-
schluss of Vienna. But these witnesses, unlike Ada Lichtman, were witnesses from before the Catastrophe.

The testimony of Ada Lichtman began with a mix-
up over her first name. In another context this might
have been humorous, but it can also be interpreted as
confusion about her identity. When the presiding judge
asked her name, she replied:

Eda Lichtman, excuse me, Ada.
PRESIDING JUDGE: Eda in Hebrew, or Ada?
WITNESS LICHTMAN: Yes, in Hebrew, Ada.
PRESIDING JUDGE: And what is it in Yiddish?
WITNESS LICHTMAN: In Yiddish, it's Ethel.
PRESIDING JUDGE: Ethel, fine. Ada, or Eda, Ethel.[36]

At the beginning of the war, Ada Lichtman lived in
Wieliczka, fourteen kilometers from Krakow, where she
had been born and had attended school. The Germans
invaded the village, rounded up all the Jewish men, beat

them, and forced them to clean the streets. Then they made them undress. "The Jewish men were forced to run with pails, and when a Jew stopped the bayonet would hit him in his back, so that almost all the men came home with blood running from them, and my father was one of them."[37] A few days later, on September 12, 1939, the German army evacuated the market square. A truck arrived and eleven officers and helmeted soldiers in green uniforms got out. It was the SS.

> Witness Lichtman: The Germans went from one dwelling to another and took out the Jews from their homes, they did not select any particular age, from fourteen up. . . . And all of them were lined up in the marketplace of Wieliczka. They were told to fold their hands behind the neck. . . .
>
> Attorney General: How many Jewish men were taken?
>
> A: Thirty-two.
>
> Q: And also Polish men?
>
> A: Later on they caught men of the intelligentsia, a high school teacher, a priest, an officer. Four men. . . . And then they were marched to the marketplace with their hands on their necks and were forced to shout, "We are traitors to the people." . . . After that they loaded them onto the truck and drove away.[38]

Ada and her sister-in-law ran after the truck, following it to a small forest where they found bodies riddled with bullets. A few weeks later, the young girl fled to Krakow, then to Mielec where she was again an eyewitness to atrocities. Jews, mainly men, were locked into the main synagogue and shot. In the streets, men with beards were rounded up and taken to the barber, where their beards where hacked off along with pieces of flesh. In 1941 Mielec was emptied of Jews. The Jews were pulled from their homes. The sick, those who could not move, were shot. The others were assembled in the market square. Young men were separated from women, old men, and children, who were taken a few kilometers away to an aviation factory. Then Ada was sent to a new camp, where she again witnessed identical scenes in the village of Dubinka: "They drove together some twenty religious Jews, clad in the clothes of the religious, long caftans, with prayer shawls and prayer books in their hands. They ordered all of them to sing religious songs and to pray, to raise their hands to God, and then some German officers came up and poured kerosene or petroleum over them and set them on fire with the prayer shawls, everything." "This you saw yourself?" the prosecutor asked. "Yes, I saw it with my own eyes." She went on to relate another episode. "An old man was carrying a child in his arms. The Germans ordered him to put the child on the ground. He told them the child could not walk. And they first shot the grandfather. I can still hear the child who was crying, 'Kill me, but don't touch my grandfather.' But they first shot the grandfather and afterwards the child."[39]

The testimony of Ada Lichtman is rarely remembered. It is usually not considered one of the highlights of the trial. Haïm Gouri, an Israeli poet and journalist and the author of *Facing the Glass Booth: The Jerusalem Trial of Adolf Eichmann,* was not present during her testimony and does not even mention her name. She is barely mentioned in studies of the trial. Her testimony

paled in comparison with that of later witnesses.
Nonetheless, as Lawrence Douglas notes, her testimony
marks a rupture in the trial.[40] This was a linguistic rupture first of all, for when the presiding judge asked her
if she spoke Hebrew, she replied that she didn't "speak
well" and that she would prefer to speak in Yiddish. The
court took her preference into account and decided that
questions would be put to her directly in Yiddish. "Suddenly, the language of the exterminated Jewish population of Europe filled the courtroom," Douglas remarks.
"As one observer commented, 'You shivered on hearing
the words of the language of the slaughtered and the
burned.'"[41] How can we not recall Sutzkever? "May
my mother tongue triumph at Nuremberg as a symbol
of perdurance," he had written in his journal, before being required to testify in Russian.

Ada Lichtman's testimony also introduced another
rupture into the structure and nature of the trial. She
was not there to deliver any evidence of the guilt of the
accused—the tie between her history and Eichmann's
actions is not at all evident. Instead, she told a story with
a double aim: to recount her own survival, but, above
all, to remember the dead and how they were murdered.

Among the testimonies that made a deep impression
was that of Leon Wells-Wieliczker, who, after his immigration to the United States in 1949, had become a
renowned scientist. Wells was the only witness whose
testimony filled two days. According to Leon Poliakov,
it was "the most dramatic testimony of the trial."[42]
Wells had been assigned along with other prisoners to
dig up mass graves, to build fires and burn the bodies,

and to crush the bones and extract any valuable objects that might remain among the ashes. He was not testifying for the first time. The first account of his experiences appeared in Polish, in Łódź in 1946. After the Eichmann trial, his memoirs, all but forgotten today, appeared in the United States, then in France.[43] The value of this text for the historian is incomparable. But the physical presence of this man—"the strangest man I've ever seen in my life," according to the Israeli poet Haim Gouri— his behavior, the tone of his voice, added something to his testimony over and above the facts. Gouri specifies that he spoke in broken English with a Polish accent, and that his was "a language without adjectives . . . as if he were creating an abstraction of himself, as if he were actually somewhere else and the person speaking only a stand-in. It was this person, not he, who had belonged to Death Brigade 1005."[44]

Another witness, Georges Wellers, had also written a book after his return from Auschwitz.[45] Both in court and in his written testimony, he described how he had witnessed the arrival at the Drancy camp of children who had been arrested on July 16 and 17, 1942, as part of the roundup at the Vélodrome d'hiver. These children and their mothers were detained at the Vélodrome for some time, then transferred to the Loiret, Pithiviers, and Beaune-la-Rolande camps. Pierre Laval, the French premier under the German Occupation, had requested permission to deport the children along with their mothers, but the response to his request was slow to arrive. The women therefore departed first, leaving their children in infinite distress. The children were then transferred to

Drancy, then deported. The devastating story of the arrival of these children at Drancy, a story that also inspired André Schwartz-Bart in *The Last of the Just,* is what Georges Wellers recounted to the court in Jerusalem. Although his words were close to those in his book, the legal setting, together with the radio—and, in the United States, television—broadcast, amplified his testimony, giving it a resonance infinitely greater than that of a limited edition book.

A last example is the testimony of Ka-tzetnik (his sobriquet meant "prisoner" in the language of the concentration camps), whose real name was Yehiel Dinor or Dinenberg. He had already testified in the postwar period, in Yiddish, and had written a memoir, *House of Dolls,*[46] which had been a best seller in the United States but did not sell well in France. When Gideon Hausner asked about his name, he replied: "It was not a pen name. I do not regard myself as a writer and a composer of literary material. This is a chronicle of the planet of Auschwitz. I was there for about two years. Time there was not like it is here on earth. Every fraction of a minute there passed on a different scale of time. And the inhabitants of this planet had no names, they had no parents nor did they have children. . . . They breathed according to different laws of nature; they did not live— nor did they die—according to the laws of this world. Their name was the number 'Kazetnik.'"[47] Hausner then interrupted him and showed him an inmate's uniform. "This is the garb of the planet called Auschwitz," replied the witness, "and I believe with perfect faith that I have to continue to bear this name so long as the world has not been aroused after this crucifixion of a nation to wipe out this evil, in the same way as humanity was aroused after the crucifixion of one man. I believe with perfect faith that, just as in astrology the stars influence our destiny, so does this planet of ashes, Auschwitz, stand in opposition to our planet earth, and influences it."[48] After a few more words, the witness fainted. The scene of his fainting is the clip of the trial most often shown in television broadcasts dealing with the Eichmann trial.

One could thus "line up" the transnational witnesses of the genocide and study the ways their testimonies have migrated from their first forms, in books or in depositions preserved in various archives, to their current forms. For instance, three figures in Claude Lanzmann's *Shoah*—Simon Srebnik, the boy singer, and Mordechai Podklebnik, two of only three people to survive Chelmno; and Itzhak Zuckermann, a hero of the Warsaw ghetto uprising—had all previously served as witnesses in the Eichmann trial.

I had thought to compare the testimonies of Simon Srebnik and Michael Podklebnik during the Eichmann trial and in Lanzmann's film. But this comparison proved almost impossible, and ultimately without interest. This was, first, because only stenographic transcripts and no film of the Eichmann trial were available to me at the time.[49] The voices and faces were missing, so that my reading of the transcripts was contaminated by the faces, voices, and, in the case of Michael Podklebnik, the flavor of Yiddish as they appeared in Lanzmann's film. In their factual elements, the stories were

the same. At the Eichmann trial, Simon Srebnik describes how one Saturday in 1943 he was walking with
his father in the Łódź ghetto and heard a gunshot. His
father fell down beside him. He was thirty years old. He
was then taken to the camp at Chelmno. When he got
out of the truck, his legs were put in chains. He wore
those chains until the liberation in 1945. "I could not
walk—I only moved my feet; we jumped."[50] Then he
describes the gas vans and the cremation of the bodies
and the experience of being shot, though the bullet did
not hit his vital organs. In his testimony at the Eichmann
trial, Srebnik does not mention singing at any point,
whereas to viewers of *Shoah,* Srebnik is the "boy
singer."

The nature of a testimony is determined both by how
an interview is conducted and by how the witness un-
derstands the questions. The prosecutor Gideon Hausner asked precise questions that called for factual
answers. Lanzmann's questions are of a different sort.
Thus he asks Michael Podklebnik: "What died in him
at Chelmno?" "Does he think it's good to talk about it?"
"Then why is he talking about it?"[51] These questions
set in motion a double reflection, absent from the Eichmann trial, in which the witness attempts to remember
what he was thinking or feeling at the time and to re-
flect on what he is feeling today. The witness is the
bearer of an experience that, albeit unique, does not exist on its own, but only in the testimonial situation in
which it takes place. It must be recognized that, in a way,
Shoah revolutionized testimony. It transformed it into

something beyond the history of historians, into a work of art.

□ □ □

Every era finds a different material support for testimony: paper, videotape, court of justice, documentary. Even when the story remains identical in its factual components, it is shaped by collective considerations, by the circumstances surrounding the act of bearing witness. It becomes part of a larger story, part of a social construct, as the Eichmann trial demonstrates with particular clarity.

The trial in Jerusalem was in theory the trial of a perpetrator. But Eichmann quickly disappeared. The attention of the media was no longer directed at the protagonist of the "final solution." The man in the glass cage was eclipsed by the victims. On May 2, 1961, Haim Gouri stated with astonishment, "Suddenly I realized that today I had not once looked into the glass booth. The events being described were larger than he was, although he had been one of those who had made them loom so large."[52] A U.S. director, Leo Horwitz, was commissioned to film the trial. He installed four hidden cameras in the courtroom to ensure uninterrupted filming of the entire trial from a single angle. The same technique was used at the Nuremberg trial. But the television audiences of the world wanted only the moments when the surviving witnesses testified.[53] It mattered little whether there was a direct link between the accused, whose presence had been eclipsed, and the events described by the witness. The witnesses spoke and it was impossible to make them abridge their stories. This was because, as Tom Segev observes, "It was not the mass-murder policy that was at the center of their stories, not the general organization or the time-tables of the trains for which Eichmann was responsible, but the terrors of death itself."[54] The witnesses told their own stories and that is what gave weight to their words. The extraordinary force their words acquired can also be attributed the place where they were pronounced, which gave them a political and social significance no book could confer. Their political dimension lay in the fact that the state, represented by the prosecutor, underwrote their testimony and thus lent it all the weight of the state's legitimacy and institutional and symbolic power. The witnesses' words attained a social dimension because they were uttered before judges whose responsibility it was to acknowledge the truth they contained and because they were relayed to the world media as a whole. For the first time since the end of the war, the witnesses had the feeling that they were being heard. As soon as the indictment was read, Haim Gouri grasped the ways that the judicial setting transformed the words pronounced there:

> They say, rightly, that the opening statement of the prosecutor, Attorney General Gideon Hausner, was an unforgettable event. I can vouch for that; I was there. Had I simply read about the things he described in any of the many books about that era, I'm afraid I would have understood them only at some remove, rather than from within. These things are well known, but

his having spoken about them in a courtroom, in Jerusalem, gave the bare facts a wondrous and unexpected power.

We can assume, therefore, that the occasion was in his favor. The mute audience, the cameras, the furious scribbling of the pencils, the people hurrying in and out, the policemen, the frozen expression on the faces of the three judges, the bailiff standing to one side—all transformed what he said into something quite different.[55]

The litany of testimonies was the essence of the Eichmann trial. "One hundred and eleven witnesses, an endless procession now receding from view, sinking and rising in a miasma of blood and smoke. One hundred and eleven proxies, each taking his or her turn on the witness stand and leading us across the desolate landscape."[56] Some specialists complained about the excessive number of witnesses called, about the length of their testimony, and, finally, about the length of the trial itself. But, as Gouri explains, the number of witnesses alone could provide an image of those years, of the "length and breadth of that world that was and is no longer."[57] He returns repeatedly to the importance of these testimonies. "Nor did the numerous witnesses come to add to the accumulation of suffering and rage. They testified in order to illuminate the destruction in all its detail. . . . They were the very center of the trial, because they served as faithful proxies of the Holocaust. They were the facts."[58] When the last witness spoke, the prosecutor informed the court that he was being bombarded with hundreds of requests from people who wished to testify. The presiding judge confirmed this. The court was bombarded with similar requests. "And you know that each of those who has asked to speak has a story that simply must be told, that at the prosecutor's door stands a long line of people pushing noisily toward the front, saying, 'What could you possibly know?' and 'You haven't heard what they did to me!' and 'Oh, what they did to us!'"[59]

Is it the function of a trial, while judging a man, to seek to retrace history? Questions have often been raised about the status of a judicial enterprise that posits an end other than its own. But no one asks about what repercussions a legal proceeding that seeks to write history has for the writing of history, nor about what it means to write a history based solely on testimonies—on testimonies that express so much suffering that nobody, not even the lawyer for the defense, Dr. Servatius, dared criticize them. He rarely objected, and then only timidly, to their relevance to the trial. Hannah Arendt offers some sensible remarks on this question. Most of the witnesses, she notes, did not possess "the rare capacity for distinguishing between things that had happened to the storyteller more than sixteen, and sometimes twenty, years ago and what he had read and heard and imagined in the meantime."[60] Above all, she denounces the right of witnesses to describe events unrelated to the charges. Indeed, the majority of the witnesses (fifty-three) came from Poland and Lithuania, territories over which Eichmann had little jurisdiction or authority. When Dr. Servatius dared at times to call attention to the fact that their testimony was in some sense "off topic," he did so discreetly, without ever discussing the actual content of the testimony, without ever interrupting the witness. Others, however, did speak out against the mixing of genres, notably Hannah Arendt, whose reports in the *New Yorker,* published in book form in 1963, led to major controversies. She rails against the fact that history, in the spirit of the indictment, was at the center of the trial, and cites Ben-Gurion: "It is not an individual that is in the dock at this historic trial, and not the Nazi regime alone, but anti-Semitism throughout history."[61] Her conclusion is definitive: "Despite the intentions of Ben-Gurion and all the efforts of the prosecution, there remained an individual in the dock, a person of flesh and blood; and if Ben-Gurion did 'not care what verdict is delivered against Eichmann,' it was undeniably the sole task of the Jerusalem court to deliver one."[62]

The Eichmann trial freed the victims to speak. It created a social demand for testimonies, just as other trials would later do in France—the trials of Klaus Barbie, of Paul Touvier, and of Maurice Papon—and just as two fictional films would do, the U.S. television miniseries *Holocaust* and Steven Spielberg's *Schindler's List.* Does this liberation of speech have a therapeutic function, as a certain psychoanalytic doctrine suggests? I do not have the expertise to decide this question, and it may well be that the effects differ depending on the individual. Among the survivors of Auschwitz who wrote books of fundamental importance, Jean Améry, an Austrian-born Belgian, Tadeuz Borowski from Poland, and the Italian Primo Levi all committed suicide, as did Piotr Rawicz, who immigrated to France after the war.

In contrast, with the Eichmann trial the survivors acquired the social identity of survivors because society now recognized them as such. Before the Eichmann trial, the survivors, as least those who so desired, maintained this identity in and for the organizations they themselves had formed. These organizations created a communal life closed in on itself, serving both to honor the memory of the dead and to maintain social ties among people who had lived through the same experiences, who considered themselves *Landsmanshaftn*, people coming from the same "land." The rare attempts to bring the memory of the genocide into the public sphere were destined to fail: politicians in every nation were against it; no segment of society demanded it. The Eichmann trial changed matters. At the heart of this newly recognized identity of the survivor was a new function: to be the bearer of history. And the advent of the witness profoundly transformed the very conditions for writing the history of the genocide. With the Eichmann trial, the witness became an embodiment of memory [*un homme-mémoire*], attesting to the past and to the continuing presence of the past. Concurrently, the genocide came to be defined as a succession of individual experiences with which the public was supposed to identify. Whereas Nuremberg sought to cast light on the perpetrators and on the mechanisms that generated the war, and sought to criminalize war and its instigators—to cast them as war criminals—the spotlight was now exclu-

sively on the victims. Whereas Nuremberg sought to in-
tervene in history by establishing the principle that political actors can be judged and by attempting to create
a new basis for international law, the Eichmann trial un-
dertook to create a memory rich in lessons for the present and the future. The functions assigned to testimony
at the Eichmann trial, clearly articulated by the Israeli
prosecutor, persist to this day, although at the time of
the trial nothing was said about what it might mean to
identify with individual experiences, or about what effects this identification might have on the behavior and
thoughts of later generations.

Nonetheless, historians of the genocide, until the appearance of Daniel Goldhagen's *Hitler's Willing Executioners,* sought to obey several fundamental rules of the
historian's profession, no matter what historiographical
perspective was chosen. After the war, two historiographical currents emerged, running parallel to each
other and keeping two histories of the Holocaust separate from each other. On one side, there was a historiography of the "final solution," that is, of the Nazi
death machine; on the other side, there was a history
of the *Hurbn,* that is, a history written from the point
of view of the victims.[63] But the historians, no matter
how they may have been personally implicated in events
contemporary to them, as were such pioneers as Leon
Poliakov, Raul Hilberg, Lucy Dawidowicz, and Saul
Friedländer, nonetheless respected the elementary rules
of the profession. They stopped short of assuming the
role of judge or prosecutor. They purposefully did not
play to the emotions and sought to construct narratives

that would appeal primarily to the intelligence. Thus Poliakov explains the problems he had writing *Harvest of Hate*: "How to find the proper tone, how to express an indignation that nonetheless had to remain secondary? The primary consideration had to be to avoid invectives, and to let the documents speak for themselves: they were sufficiently eloquent."[64] Contrary to what Hausner or Hartman claim, history written in this way is not "in cold storage." Holding events at a distance does not preclude feelings of empathy with the victims or horror at the complex system that produced mass death. It restores the dignity of the thinking person, a dignity that Nazism had precisely derided by playing on feelings such as hate or on emotions such as those generated at mass rallies.

Daniel Goldhagen's work pulverized the universally established criteria for the academic writing of history. In this sense, it is a symptom of a crisis in the field of history at the present time. This crisis manifests itself first in connection with the genocide of the Jews but also affects other areas, such as the history of communism or of the Resistance. In effect, the posture adopted by Goldhagen and accepted by the U.S. academics who conferred his doctoral degree, mirrors the position of Gideon Hausner to a surprising extent.

Daniel Goldhagen announced it up front. He is hostile to "mere clinical descriptions of the killing operations," to "antiseptic descriptions," which he considers sins against what he calls "the phenomenology of killing." Phenomenology is a philosophical term, but here

it designates what would otherwise be simply called
"description." In Goldhagen's terms, Gideon Hausner
was doing phenomenology without knowing it. There is
a constant discrepancy in Goldhagen's work between
the crudeness of his account, the simplicity of his pro-
nouncements, and the theoretical façade surrounding
them. Goldhagen wants to avoid "the clinical approach
and try to convey the horror, the gruesomeness, of the
events *for the perpetrators.*" He specifies: "Blood, bone,
and brains were flying about, often landing on the kil-
lers, smirching their faces and staining their clothes.
Cries and wails of people awaiting their imminent
slaughter or consumed in death throes reverberated in
German ears. Such scenes—not the antiseptic description that mere reportage of a killing operation presents—constituted the reality for many perpetrators.
For us to comprehend the perpetrators' phenomenological world, we should describe for ourselves every gruesome image that they beheld, and every cry of anguish
and pain that they heard."[65] One cannot help but think
that the author has exceeded the task assigned to the
historian. How do these images, these cries, form in the
mind? What mental landscape is available to him, from
what stock of images or sounds can he draw to enrich
his descriptions, since he was not there—unless he is
drawing on images formed during his childhood in the
United States, that is, images stored in his imagination
from films and television programs depicting violence,
which probably fed his imagination? How do we know,
for instance, that the victims cried out in anguish and

pain? Do anguish and fear always express themselves in cries? Could there not be at times, to borrow the title of a novel by Henri Raczymow, a "cry without a voice"?[66]

The author then turns to his conception of history. "The discussion of any killing operation, of any single death, should be replete with such descriptions. This, of course, cannot be done, because it would make any study of the Holocaust unacceptably lengthy, and also because few readers would be able to persevere in reading through the gruesome accounts—such inability itself being a powerful commentary on the extraordinary phenomenology of the perpetrators' existence and the powerful motivations that must have impelled Germans to silence such emotions so that they could kill and torture Jews, including children, as they did."[67]

Goldhagen's conception of history is strange and recalls the ideas that led Hausner to call witnesses to the stand. History in this view is the juxtaposition of horror stories. The ideal history—unrealizable because it would be at once intolerable and too long—would be the individualized story of each of the six million murders. Besides the fact that Goldhagen's conception of the history of the genocide—and this has been remarked by some historians—does not account for "industrial" murder, for the gas vans and gas chambers, where the executioner is at a remove from the victim and kills at a distance, one might wonder what the heuristic value of such a history is, or simply whether the absence of the desire to think in more general terms is not in effect the very negation of history. It would signify the death of the intellectual operation that consists in constructing a story and which is called, precisely, the writing of history. In place of a narrative that seeks both to establish the facts of the past and to give them meaning, there would be other, individual narratives privileging horror. The historians of World War I, in this light, could tell us stories about the horror of life in the trenches; the Chinese could tell us how the Japanese invaders committed a massacre by bayonet during the siege of Nanking. Historical explanation would be reduced to the simplest terms, as it is in Goldhagen's work. "People must be motivated to kill others, or else they would not do so."[68] This claim does not depend on any argument and its logic is superficial. Over the course of the centuries, there has been much killing, but I am not sure, especially during wars, that those who killed had strong motives. Above all, the conception of history that is expressed by Goldhagen encourages the abandonment of thought and intelligence in favor of sentiment and emotion.

Moreover, and this again links Goldhagen and Hausner, whereas Goldhagen is supposedly interested in the perpetrators, it is in fact to the victims' stories that he most often appeals. Goldhagen's method is particularly clear in the section of his book devoted to the death marches. He describes to us the suffering of the prisoners forced to march in a state of total exhaustion, abused and starved, while the Reich is on the verge of collapse. According to Goldhagen, the only motivation for their murders was a deliberate desire to kill, and he invites us to put ourselves in the position of the perpetrators. This is an impossible position to occupy. No reader can imagine herself capable of such cruelty—unless, of course, she feels a perverse pleasure in the description of the humiliation and execution of the victims, a pleasure we cannot entirely discount. Just as, at the Eichmann trial, the stories of the witnesses sufficed to make Eichmann's guilt apparent, the "phenomenological" descriptions of the horror serve to establish that ordinary Germans, moved by a secular anti-Semitism that Goldhagen calls "eliminationist," were, as the title of his book indicates, "Hitler's willing executioners." Here again, Goldhagen is close to Hausner, who suggested that "perhaps [Eichmann] was only an innocent executor of some mysteriously foreordained destiny, or, for that matter, even of anti-Semitism."[69]

Finally, one last point: the tone adopted by Goldhagen is that of a prosecutor. Marc Bloch observed that historians have always been tempted to succumb to "that satanic enemy of true history, the mania of judgment." For him, the historian's categorical imperative is to understand and to explain, not to deliver peremptory judgment. Hence Bloch's well-known phrase: "Robespierrists! Anti-Robespierrists! For pity's sake, simply tell us what Robespierre was!"[70] As concerns the history of Nazism—and the history of communism as well—it seems that this injunction has lost its relevance and that historians have renounced the difficult, thankless, and probably futile (but so what!) task of trying to understand. It may have lost its relevance furthermore because the historian has worked and works in the legal climate that contaminates all of society. The great trial at Nuremberg allowed an impressive quantity of documents to be brought to light. In this sense, it served historians. The polemics that followed the Eichmann trial gave historical research a decisive push, though this major aspect of the trial, the advent of the figure of the witness, has not been perceived. Goldhagen's work belongs to the aftermath of the Eichmann trial. We are left to wonder, along with Raul Hilberg, whether this work, in which the "intricate apparatus" is replaced with "rifles, whips and fists"—and, we might add, with the display of the victims' suffering—constitutes a "transitory event or a lasting addition to the literature,"[71] in an epoch when, in a global fashion, individual stories and personal opinion often take the place of analysis.

III

THE ERA OF THE WITNESS

Toward the end of the 1970s, the systematic collection of audiovisual testimonies began. The global context had changed. The genocide of the Jews was now a strong presence in political life in France, Israel, and the United States. But Western societies had also changed, and these changes could not but affect the very nature of testimony. Testimony projects and archives proliferated. In an article in *Le Monde*, Frédéric Gaussen observed:

> To tell one's life story is a satisfaction refused only with difficulty. It is the proof that one has in truth existed, and that an interlocutor is there, ready to take an interest in you. Persons of importance—and indeed, those of less importance—have always longed to address others by writing their memoirs. Others, ordinary people, satisfied themselves with the more limited public of family and friends.
>
> But such relative differences among individual des-

tinies can no longer be taken for granted. The idea has
taken hold that all lives equally deserve to be told.[1]

The 1970s and early 1980s witnessed an extraordinary
craze for ethnological "life stories"—the Breton fisher-
man, the retired schoolteacher, and so on. In a way, at
issue was a democratization of historical actors, an attempt to give voice to the excluded, the unimportant,
the voiceless. In the context of the post-1968 years, it
was also a political act. The mass demonstrations in
France in May 1968 were characterized by a massive effort to seize control of public discourse. In their wake,
this phenomenon spread not only to the humanities and
social sciences but also to the media—radio and television—which began increasingly to seek out the man in
the street.

The 1970s were also a time when feelings and psychological problems began to be exhibited publicly, first
through radio, then television. In the early 1990s, a new
kind of television show appeared in France, modeled on
U.S. shows and based on the language of ordinary people. This eruption of profane experience and of private
testimony into the public sphere emblematizes what the
sociologist Dominique Mehl calls the television of intimacy. It was also in the 1970s that the ideology of human rights triumphed. Every society, every historical
period came to be measured by the degree of respect it
gave to human rights. The individual was thus placed at
the heart of society and, retrospectively, of history. The
individual and the individual alone became the public
embodiment of history.

At the end of the 1970s, after the emotional reactions and controversies that followed the broadcast of the television miniseries *Holocaust* in the United States as well as in France and Germany, the idea emerged for the first time that it was necessary to record video testimonies of those the Americans call "survivors," those who lived under Nazi domination in the Third Reich or in the countries occupied by the Nazis and who escaped the Final Solution. This is clearly a broad definition because it includes not only the direct victims—those who were interned in the various camps or in the ghettos— but also persons whose lives were certainly threatened but who did not necessarily suffer directly in the flesh.

The televised miniseries *Holocaust* was a prodigious success first in the United States, drawing 120 million viewers. In Germany, where it aired next, it produced a profound reaction. A critic noted: "Germany has been enriched by a new American word 'Holocaust,' which simultaneously covers the Jewish genocide, the TV movie and its personalized tragedy, and the emotional and political reactions it promoted."[2] French television at first resisted purchasing the miniseries for broadcast. It was too expensive. Moreover, France had already produced something superior, Alain Resnais's *Night and Fog*. Finally, Claude Lanzmann was working on a film and it seemed fitting to wait until it was finished. But the French television station Antenne 2 decided to buy the rights in November 1978. The miniseries was shown in February 1979 and a debate on the topic "Life and death in the Nazi death camps" immediately followed.

As in the United States and Germany, the film provoked heated debates that lasted for months.

The producer, Marvin Chomsky, whose miniseries *Roots* had already been wildly successful and who was also responsible for such shows as *Columbo* and *Mannix*, constructed the screenplay for the miniseries as four two-hour segments based on a novel by Gerald Green. The miniseries followed two German families, one won over to Nazism and the other Jewish—the Weiss family, meant to embody the fate of the German Jews. The author wanted the Weisses to be a typical middle-class family: the father a neighborhood doctor, the mother a housewife, two children. The miniseries depicts the crumbling of the family's entire value system, until the parents find no other solution than to take their own lives. Only the son, Rudi, survives, by fighting with the resistance, then leaving for Palestine.

Criticisms of the miniseries were identical in the United States, France, and Germany. It was accused of being "romanticized," "a Hollywood product." The situations dramatized by the miniseries were classic Hollywood film scenes: the forced separation of the lovers, the death of a best friend or family member, social corruption. What characterized the history of the persecution of the Jews—intolerable anguish, suffering, hunger, mass death—was not shown.

But above all, while a large number of survivors would recognize their history in Steven Spielberg's *Schindler's List*, which they would support against all criticism by intellectuals, it was certain survivors themselves who expressed the most virulent criticisms of *Holocaust*. The first of these critics was Elie Wiesel in the *New York Times*. He was severe. "Untrue, offensive, cheap: as a TV production, the film is an insult to those who perished and to those who survived. In spite of its name, this 'docu-drama' is not about what some of us remember as the Holocaust. . . . It transforms an onto-logical event into soap-opera. . . . The witness feels here duty-bound to declare: what you have seen on the screen is not what happened *there*."[3] Charlotte Delbo, who, like Marie-Claude Vaillant-Couturier, was part of the only convoy of women resistance fighters sent to Ausch-witz, had a similar impression: "When I sat down in front of the TV set, I had a lump in my throat. Based on the articles I had read I was afraid that I would feel un-controllable emotion at the sight of truly unbearable things. Almost immediately the lump disappeared. I was not moved—and I don't think that I am inured to such things because I'm an Auschwitz survivor."[4] As for Si-mone Veil, she rejected the miniseries vision of the rela-tionship among prisoners, portrayed as attentive to one other and acting in solidarity. Prisoners might have stolen the blanket of someone who died, as the series shows, but, she points out, they could also take the blan-ket from another living prisoner, which is not shown.[5]

In the United States, the reaction of "ordinary" sur-vivors—those who had not written their memoirs, who did not enjoy any celebrity, who did not speak out in newspapers or on television—was the same. "So many lost their lives, will their life story too be taken away? was the complaint. Any survivor could tell a history more true and terrible in its detail, more authentic in its depiction."[6] This multifaceted complaint deserves examination. It reveals, first, an acute anxiety that is not exclusive to survivors of the genocide: that of being dispossessed of one's history by someone outside the experience who claims to be telling it. The Weiss family could not pretend to represent all the Jewish families of Europe. In any case, the diversity of social, political, and cultural situations among European Jews in the 1930s was such that it would be fruitless to try to represent them with any single "type." Yet the type chosen, the assimilated Jew from the Western European petite bourgeoisie, was not a matter of chance. It was certainly easier for the U.S. viewer to identify with this type of person than with a Polish Jew wearing a caftan and sidelocks, the father of a large, Yiddish-speaking family. Nonetheless, many, very many, such Polish Jews perished in the genocide and indeed constituted the majority of its victims. The survivors were not the only ones dispossessed of their stories by the miniseries. Their complaint also concerned those who did not survive and whose history was stolen by *Holocaust* when they were not there to tell it themselves. Indeed, one of the recurring themes in both oral and written survivor testimony is of a promise made to a friend or relative who is about to die, a promise to tell the world what happened to them and thus to save them from oblivion—to make death a little less futile. Survival itself is often explained and justified by this will to honor the legacy of those who perished. The last argument advanced by the survivors who rejected the miniseries was that their history demanded a greater authenticity, which would come about, notably, when such films showed more of the horrors. This argument echoes the reasons given by those who sought to testify at the Eichmann trial.

One of the consequences of the television broadcast, therefore, was to elicit an ardent and quite often newly felt desire among survivors in the United States to tell their stories, as the Eichmann trial had done for survivors in Israel. Geoffrey Hartman remarks that the survivors expressed this desire to testify at a specific moment in their lives. And the end of the 1970s, these men and women were well established in the United States. They had had families, and their own children were becoming parents in turn. The chain of generations, doubly broken by the genocide and by emigration, was thus on its way to being reconstituted. The survivors no longer felt reticent about making their pasts known and about "the establishment of a legacy."[7] On the contrary, a change had taken place, one that began with the Eichmann trial. Survivors, whose stories were avoided during the postwar years, became respectable and respected persons in their very identities as survivors. Alvin Rosenfeld is probably correct in crediting Elie Wiesel with this transformation. Wiesel was certainly the first to put into words the idea that there is no shame, either collective or individual, in being a victim of the Holocaust. During a debate that took place in New York in 1967, Wiesel declared:

Why then do we admittedly think of the Holocaust with shame? Why don't we claim it as a glorious chapter in our eternal history? After all, it did change man and his world—well, it did not change man, but it did change the world. It is still the greatest event in our times. Why then are we ashamed of it? In its power it even influenced language. Negro quarters are called ghettos; Hiroshima is explained by Auschwitz; Vietnam is described in terms which were used one generation ago. Everything today revolves around our Holocaust experience. Why then do we face it with such ambiguity? Perhaps this should be the task of Jewish educators and philosophers: to reopen the event as a source of pride, to take it back into our history.

Later in the same discussion he added:

I already mentioned pride: I believe in the necessity to restore Jewish pride even in relation to the Holocaust. I do not like to think of the Jew as suffering. I prefer thinking of him as someone who can defeat suffering—his own and others'. For his is a Messianic dimension: he can save the world from a new Auschwitz. As Camus would say: one must create happiness to protest against a universe of unhappiness. But— one *must* create it. And we are creating it. We were creating it. Jews got married, celebrated weddings, had children within the ghetto walls. Their absurd faith in their non-existent future was, nevertheless, *af al pi chen,* an affirmation of the spirit. Thus, theirs is the pride, it is not ours. Not yet.[8]

Two decades after Wiesel's declarations, the change had come about. "These men and women," wrote Leon Uris, the author of the successful novels *Exodus* and

Mila 18, speaking of the survivors, "are to be looked upon with wonderment."[9] And so they were.

The U.S. political context had also changed. In 1973, for the first time, the major Jewish-American organizations included in their agendas the need to preserve the memory of the Holocaust. Publications and academic programs in universities proliferated. Whereas in 1962 only one course on the Holocaust existed, at Brandeis University, such courses became widespread. By 1995 there were more than one hundred institutions devoted to the study of the Holocaust. This was first of all a reaction, in the United States as well as in France and Israel, to the Six-Day War. During the period that preceded the Israeli victory, anxiety seized the population of Israel. This anxiety was lived in "genocidal" mode and with an almost identical intensity by U.S. and French Jews. It was feared that the state of Israel would be destroyed, and this fear brought to mind another destruction. On June 4, the eve of the outbreak of war, Raymond Aron, who was usually little inclined to intimate revelations, wrote: "An irresistible sense of solidarity is seizing hold of us; what matter where it comes from. If the superpowers, following the cold calculation of their interests, allow the destruction of the small state of Israel, this crime, modest on a global scale, will leave me without the will to live, even though it is not my country. Millions of men, I believe, will be ashamed of humanity." A few months later, he added: "I know also, more clearly than yesterday, that the possibility of the destruction of the state of Israel [which would be accompanied by the massacre of part of its population] wounds me to the bottom of my soul."[10] Aron called this possible destruction "state-cide."

Raymond Aron was not alone in his anxiety about a possible new destruction, just as he was far from the only one to become aware of a sense of belonging. French Jews, whatever their affiliation with community organizations, shared this experience. Thus Richard Marienstras explained during a roundtable organized by the journal *Esprit*:

> The solidarity that is manifested [with respect to the state of Israel]—and that sometimes becomes an object of conscious reflection—is not based on the defense of a form of government or of any particular politics. It is manifested so vividly because everyone felt that, beneath the political body and government, what was threatened was an original community that had formed a state to survive and to perpetuate or deepen its culture. We all felt that the threat weighing on Israel was not a political threat but an ontological one, aimed at the physical and cultural being of Israel, aimed at the destruction of its inhabitants, of the state, of the collectivity. In short, what we feared was a cultural genocide, as well as a genocide plain and simple.[11]

Similarly, Wladimir Rabi spoke of "the impossibility of imagining a second Auschwitz during the same generation."[12]

The Six-Day War, then the 1973 war, also had another, paradoxical effect for U.S. Jews. Zionism, which during the years of the war and afterward had acted as a powerful bond, orienting the identities of nonreligious Jews, became more problematic, more conflictual. Israel was no longer a utopia but had become a real country occupying territories conquered in the Six-Day War. With Israel's intervention in Libya and with the intifada, the unanimity of the Jewish world with respect to Israel was ruptured. The heart of Jewish identity shifted imperceptibly from absolute support of and identification with Israel to the revitalization of the memory of the genocide. On the political front, Jimmy Carter's actions were decisive. When the U.S. president declared the need to work toward establishing a Palestinian state and demanded that Israel reinstate the borders in place before the Six-Day War, he precipitated a crisis in his relations with the U.S. Jewish community, which, since Franklin Delano Roosevelt, had strongly supported the Democratic Party. How could he reconcile with them during his reelection campaign?

In 1977 the United States established an organization charged with tracking down Nazi war criminals who had legally entered the country during the years following the German surrender, some of whom even later worked for the U.S. government. Additionally, a month after the broadcast of *Holocaust*, President Carter, acknowledging the emotion it had aroused, announced the creation of a presidential Holocaust commission to be chaired by Elie Wiesel, who embodied the survivor in the United States. This announcement coincided with the thirtieth anniversary of the creation of the state of Israel. It was a decisive gesture, aimed at appeasing the Jews with a view toward the next presidential election. On October 7, 1980, a law created the American Memorial Council of the Holocaust, charged with creating a national memorial. The idea came from advisers to the president. Carter was not responding to pressure from Jewish groups. It was the first significant political intervention in what until then had belonged to the private domain. From that moment on, the memory of the genocide, already a key issue for Jewish organizations, became a political theme as well.

Holocaust thus dramatically exposed the transformations taking place in the landscape of memorialization and the new elements entering that landscape: the changing image of the survivor, altered notions of Jewish identity, new political uses of the genocide. At least in France, survivors were also enlisted to authenticate the television miniseries. Before 1976, as Jacques Walter notes, there had been only six television programs on the genocide. Appearances by witnesses and survivors were "few and far between." The televised news segments devoted to *Holocaust* were no exception to this rule, since they dealt with the reception of the miniseries in Germany and with its pedagogical dimension. Survivors appeared only during a debate following the broadcast. The role they were assigned was pedagogical; they were asked to enter into dialogue with "the youth." This goal was emphasized by the seating arrangement of the debate, in which former inmates were placed across the room from the young people.[13]

□ □ □

In New Haven, Connecticut, home of Yale University, some realized that they knew practically nothing about

the survivors of the Holocaust, even though some were
their neighbors. One of these survivors was Dori Laub,
a psychiatrist and psychoanalyst who had been a child
in Romania during the war. They therefore decided
to establish a "Cinematic Project on Holocaust Survivors," assisted by the Farband, a group of survivors
from the New Haven area. By the time Yale University
offered its help and the Yale Video Archive for Holocaust Testimonies opened its doors in 1982, the project
already included some two hundred testimonies. By
1995, the Fortunoff[14] Video Archive for Holocaust
Testimonies had collected approximately 3,600 testimonies—close to 10,000 hours of interviews gathered
throughout the United States, as well as in Greece, Bo-
livia, Slovakia, Belgium, Germany, Israel, Argentina,
Serbia, Belarus, and Ukraine.[15]

What were the motivations behind the Yale Video
Archive, which demanded an immense amount of time,
energy, and, because it was decided that the filming
should be of professional quality, money? Geoffrey
Hartman explains that from the outset concern for the
survivors was behind the project, "a duty to listen and
to restore a dialogue with people so marked by their
experience that total integration into everyday life
is a semblance—though a crucial and comforting semblance."[16] Testimony was thus immediately assigned a
new function in relation to those I have already ana-
lyzed: to allow the survivor to speak. That function is
difficult to define. Is it social therapy, because it consists
of restoring a connection that had been broken? Dori
Laub, one of the project's founders, who helped develop

and was essentially responsible for the training program for interviewers, affirms: "Lying is toxic and silence suffocates. There is, in every survivor, an imperative need to *tell* and thus to come to *know* one's story, unimpeded by the ghosts from the past against which one has to protect oneself. One has to know one's buried truth in order to be able to live one's life. It is a mistake to believe that silence favors peace. The 'not telling' of the story serves as a perpetuation of its tyranny. The events become more and more distorted in their silent retention and pervasively invade and contaminate the survivor's daily life." He goes on to insist that one cannot and should not speak unless one is listened to: "The unlistened-to story is a trauma as serious as the initial event."[17]

The method of recording testimonies, developed in stages at Yale, is intimately tied to this primary objective: to give birth to a voice and to allow it to be heard. The interview takes place in a studio, that is, in a place closed off from the normal environment of the person being interviewed, so that nothing will distract him or her from delving deeply into memory and the past. The interviewers, whose training is most often supervised by a psychoanalyst and who are taught the rudiments of the history of the genocide, do not use a preestablished questionnaire. Their role is to help the witnesses keep track of the story or to assist them in recalling painful episodes when they are suffering. The interviewer is not supposed to comment on or correct the narrative. The expression of emotion is encouraged, if not incited. At least at the outset, the Yale project was a community effort, a local effort one could say, centered on the survivors themselves, toward whom those working at the Yale Archive always demonstrated the utmost respect, and on their social ties to their environment.

What Geoffrey Hartman calls a "testimonial pact" is thus created between the interviewer and the witness. Small communities are also formed comprising survivors, interviewers, and researchers interested in the material collected.

Today, the Yale Video Archive is far from unique. Various museums, memorials, and memorial associations have established their own interviewing projects. More than any other single factor, the creation of the Survivors of the Shoah Visual History Foundation established by Steven Spielberg in 1994 changed the scale of testimony collection. Jacques Walter, drawing on the writings of the project's founders, summarizes its development as follows. In 1994, while making *Schindler's List* in Poland, Spielberg was overwhelmed by the stories of the survivors working as advisers to the film, who agreed to tell their stories on camera. In an interview in the French newspaper *Libération,* Spielberg explained that he wanted "to conserve history as it is transmitted to us by those who lived through it and who managed to survive. It is essential that we see their faces, hear their voices, and understand that they are ordinary people like us who went through the atrocities of the Holocaust."[18] The project of creating an archive of survivor testimony was born, then, from the making of a film. The analogy with the Yale Archive, the creation of which was also related to a film, is troubling. Two fictional films dealing with the genocide that were seen by tens of millions, even hundreds of millions throughout the world were also at the origin of the two most important testimony archives. But whereas the survivors testified in reaction to *Holocaust,* in order to make their voices heard, one could say that they testified in symbiosis with *Schindler's List,* as a complement and not in opposition to the film. The differences do not end there. The emphasis in Spielberg's project is different from that of the Yale Archive. The person of the survivor is no longer at the center of the enterprise. The survivor has been replaced by a concept, that of transmission. Whereas the founders of the Yale Archive insisted on the survivors' sense of having lived on "another planet," as Ka-tzetnik put it at the Eichmann trial, on their sense of being forever isolated from the world and from their relatives by an extreme experience, the Spielberg project is based, conversely, on the desire to show "ordinary people," people who have returned to "normal," who have survived the shipwreck of war.

Briefly put, in contrast to the artisanal character of the Yale Archive, the Spielberg project manifests an "industrial"[19] dimension. Because the survivors were approaching death, it was necessary to interview all who could be as quickly as possible—some 300,000 in all, with a goal of 50,000 by the end of 1997 and 150,000 before 2000—and to conduct these interviews wherever the survivors were located.[20] Each team working in the various countries where survivors lived was supposed to work five days a week, conducting four interviews a day. By 1995 the Spielberg Foundation had already collected close to 20,000 testimonies in the United States, South Africa, Israel, and Europe, including 1,300 in France. The project considered yield an important measure of success. The foundation's Web site published a daily tally of the testimonies collected (42,274 on April 18, 1998) and reported the number of interviews conducted each week (198 for the week of April 11, 1998).[21] On January 12, 1998, Michael Berenbaum, president of the Spielberg Foundation, reported on the state of the archives: "If someone wanted to watch all the material we have collected, it would take nine-and-a-half years watching the tapes twenty-four hours a day. We have almost 39,000 interviews in thirty different languages. Because 20% of each story is about daily life before the Holocaust, and 15% about life after the war, we have built, for the first time, an exhaustive picture of the life of Jewish communities in the twentieth century. It is also the first time that an event is being told by those who lived through it. Normally, history relies on documents and on stories of leaders."[22]

Berenbaum's assertion cannot fail to trouble even a historian who is positively disposed toward the collection of testimonies. This is because Spielberg's ambition is to tell the history of the Holocaust, as is indicated by the name of his Visual History Foundation. In the United States, the foundation already provides pedagogical materials to secondary school teachers. But 20 percent of some 39,000 life stories collected by the Spielberg Foundation do not by any means comprise an "exhaustive picture of the life of Jewish communities in the twentieth century." As things stand, they are simply

39,000 juxtaposed versions of what the survivors remember about native communities that, for the most
part, have been erased from the map. A historian who
agreed to watch these stories day and night for two
years would at most be able to draw a picture of how
the survivors remembered their communities fifty years
after their destruction. But the historian would in no
case be able to reconstruct the history of these communities. I have already verified this in my study, conducted
with I. Niborski, of the image of lost communities
recorded in memorial books. We found that "the books
that appeared before the war, monographs devoted to
the towns of Pinsk or Vilna, expressed, though the se-
lection of texts, the desire to offer a synthetic account of
Jewish life by situating themselves in relation to the
problem of the evolution of *Yiddishkeit* in Poland or in
the emigration. The memorial books do not have any
analytical or synthetic perspective. Members of Jewish
society who were at odds or ignored each other entirely,
the assimilated or the orthodox, Bundist or communist,
boss or worker, are here simply mixed together as they
were mixed together in death."[23]

The Spielberg Foundation benefited from, and
claimed to be inspired by, the Yale project, from which
it doubtless sought a "scientific" legitimacy. But it
nonetheless substantially modified the Yale interview
technique—and, consequently, the very meaning of
the project. Potential interviewers, all volunteers, completed a questionnaire designed to test their knowledge
of the Holocaust and their general competency. Once
accepted, they underwent three days of training, at-

tending presentations on history and psychology and critiques of testimonies. After this training program, they were declared ready to interview. The foundation, which loves numbers, reported that there were 8,500 candidates for the interviewer positions, of whom 4,500 took part in the training sessions, and that 2,400 in the end conducted interviews.

Designers of the Spielberg project believe that testimony should be regulated. In principle, each testimony was to be of a fixed length, two hours; 60 percent of each session should be devoted to the war and 20 percent each to the periods before and after the war. But above all, and this is the principal innovation with respect to the interviews conducted at Yale, at the end of the interview, as in certain radio broadcasts, the survivor was supposed to deliver a message expressing "what he or she would hope to leave as a legacy for future generations." The survivor's family (spouse, children, and grandchildren are specified), though excluded from the place where the interview occurs, usually the survivor's home, was to be invited to reunite with the survivor at the end of the interview, unless the witness opposed it. The end of the interview is thus in some sense the equivalent of the epilogue to *Schindler's List*. Accompanied by the actors who played their roles in the film, the real life survivors on the list walk by Oskar Schindler's grave in the cemetery of the Mount of Olives in Jerusalem, as the number of their descendants is announced. The film, heretofore in black and white, changes to color. *Schindler's List* thus has a happy ending. A single individual, one of the Righteous among the

Nations, sufficed to annul the Destruction. In the same way, the interviewed survivors show their happy lives after so many trials. The message is optimistic: the family, reconstituted thanks to their descendants, is the living proof of the Nazis' failure to exterminate a people. This message reveals the true nature of these interviews. The project is not ultimately concerned with constructing an oral history of the Holocaust but rather with creating an archive of survival.

The modifications introduced by the Spielberg project are magnified by the onerous logistical demands involved in video testimony. Whereas the interviewers and the staff of the Yale Archive are volunteers, with the exception of a handful of paid staff members who work on video conservation, cataloging, and the general operation of the archive, the Spielberg project has a staff of more than 240 full-time employees, and its interviewers receive a stipend.[24] Contrary to common belief, the project is not financed by profits from *Schindler's List*, that is, by Spielberg's money. Rather, Steven Spielberg created a foundation whose budget—some 60 million dollars in the three years from 1995 to 1998— comes from Steven Spielberg, MCA-Universal, NBC, the Wasserman Foundation, and Time Warner. Thus, the funds the Spielberg Foundation receives might have gone to other projects related to the memory of the genocide, notably the Fortunoff Archive. Whereas the Yale interviews were largely nondirective and open-ended, those conducted by the Spielberg teams were directed and limited to two hours, following a common protocol in all the countries where interviews took place. The videos were then sent to Los Angeles to be digitized and indexed. On the technological cutting edge, these digitized testimonies are supposed to become available on a server, so that the young people whom the Spielberg project hopes to educate can consult extracts from these testimonies on their computer screens with the help of an index. They will also be able to consult all sorts of related information: the witness's family archives, photos related to the events the witness describes, a map indicating the site of the camp or ghetto in question, and so on.

It is clear that we have come a long way from the clandestine writings of the ghettos, composed in an eradicated language, often buried underground, which came down to us by such hazardous and difficult routes. What will the testimonial landscape look like if and when new technologies of dissemination become ubiquitous? What vision of the Holocaust will those born three generations from now have? No one can tell. Only one thing seems certain. Lamenting the limits of the academic history of the Shoah—too cerebral, too cold—Geoffrey Hartman hoped that the stories of the survivors would be heard, stories whose eminently literary qualities he highlighted. This hardly seems scandalous to me, since historical interpretation has never pretended to any hegemony. Michael Berenbaum and Steven Spielberg, however, seek something entirely different: the substitution of testimonies, supposedly real history, for the history of historians. It is quite simply a historiographical revolution to which we are invited, a revolution made possible by modern technology. History would thus be returned to its true authors, those to whom it belongs: the actors and witnesses who tell it directly, for present and future listeners.

In April 1998, the database of the Spielberg Foundation included only 1,600 testimonies. But the catalog is a work in progress. Michael Berenbaum explains: "We are preparing materials for teachers who *still use books* [my emphasis], but who in five years will all be connected to computer networks, at least in the United States. We have created a new digital catalog using key words and will also be producing CD-ROMs, documentaries, and books."[25] A cultural revolution is combined with the historiographical one: the written word in teaching is abandoned in favor of "modern" technologies.

It would be a mistake to see only the technical aspects of the problem. The Spielberg collection is part of a larger movement that Michael Berenbaum calls "the Americanization of the Holocaust." The expression is valorizing in its intention. It designates the transplantation of an event from the place where it occurred, Europe, to the United States, as well as the modifications this entails. He explains:

> The Holocaust is now part of Western culture and, in America, it represents the absolute experience. People don't know what good and evil are, but they are certain about one thing: the Holocaust is absolute evil. On television, *Schindler's List* was seen in sixty-five million homes. It was the largest audience in the history of American television for a non-sports program three-and-a-half hours long. . . . And of the ten million people who have already visited the Holocaust

Memorial, the new museum in Washington, only 20 percent have been Jewish. This is why I have coined the term, *the Americanization of the Holocaust*. We have taken a European event and integrated it into American culture, popular culture. Today, the event is understood differently in Washington, Warsaw, Paris, and Jerusalem.

Young African Americans leaving the museum in Washington often say, "We didn't know the Jews were *black*." It took me a long time to understand that for them the face of suffering was black even if the victims were white. In the United States, the Holocaust is used to teach traditional American values: to remind us first that all people are created equal, with inalienable rights that the state cannot take away. It is seen as the extreme expression of something that is ultimately, in fact, ordinary. This is contrary to Elie Wiesel's definition of the Holocaust as a world apart, not belonging to our world. In the United States, it serves now as an example to justify efforts to limit government intervention.[26]

This is an extraordinary declaration, and it is not isolated. A French reader imbued with the culture emerging from the Cold War, when American civilization was readily demonized, may see the concept of the "Americanization of the Holocaust" in negative terms. But Michael Berenbaum in no way means it pejoratively. What he describes is a variegated reality that can be summarized by the fact that the United States is currently at the center of the Holocaust. Holocaust historiography, having once been German and Israeli, is now principally American. The Holocaust Memorial Museum in Washington, D.C., has undertaken the gigantic

task of microfilming all the archives related to the genocide of the Jews across the globe: not only those of the
former Soviet states, which have been inaccessible until
now, but also Western European archives already familiar to historians. Thus the French archives, those
conserved in private centers such as the Center for the
Documentation of Contemporary Jewry (CDJC) and
those in public archives, will be accessible in Washington. It will thus become more convenient to travel to the
United States, where the totality of the archives will be
available, than to take archival research trips across
France and Europe. In 1953 the CDJC had just placed
the first stone for the first memorial—which was supposed to be a world memorial—to those who died in the
Shoah. In response, and following violent arguments
with the CDJC, the Knesset approved a law creating
Yad Vashem and affirming the centrality of Israel in
the memory and history of the genocide. Yad Vashem
sought to be the sole central repository for the names of
the dead; it authorized the construction of memorials; it
centralized the archives. But it seems that the provisions
of that law are now obsolete. Yad Vashem's resources
are derisory compared with those of the United States.

But the "Americanization of the Holocaust"[27] cannot be reduced to a mere change in the location of the
institutions that produce history and memory. It also
generates its own vision of the Holocaust, a vision that
has been exported widely, mainly in films. Alvin Rosenfeld points out a paradox: recent surveys aimed at as-
sessing knowledge of the genocide of the Jews show that
Americans, compared to the French, English, and Ger-

mans, are by far the most ignorant, while at the same time it is in the United States, to all appearances at least, that the Holocaust is most palpably present. A single example: only 21 percent of Americans realize that the Warsaw ghetto has a connection to the Holocaust.

Rosenfeld also observes that in the United States most people see Nazi war crimes less through the lens of historical accounts than through images and stories produced by popular writers, artists, and film producers. To recall the role of *Holocaust* and *Schindler's List:* "It is part of the American ethos to stress goodness, innocence, optimism, liberty, diversity, and equality. It is part of the same ethos to downplay or deny the dark and brutal sides of life and instead to place a preponderant emphasis on the saving power of individual moral conduct and collective deeds of redemption. Americans prefer to think affirmatively and progressively. The tragic vision, therefore, is antithetical to the American way of seeing the world, according to which people are meant to overcome adversity and not cling endlessly to their sorrows."[28] The U.S. view Rosenfeld describes clashes with that formed by a historian studying the genocide of the Jews.

The genocide was absent from political life in the United States and elsewhere until the beginning of the 1960s. It was also absent from cultural life. Of the five hundred or so films produced by Hollywood, "We find striking avoidance of any explicit presentation of the Jewish catastrophe during the course of the war."[29] Hollywood only broke this silence in 1959 with the filming of *The Diary of Anne Frank.*

Much can be said about the importance of Anne Frank's diary in forming the memory of the genocide. But I am far from sure that the adolescents, girls especially, who read the book emerge informed about the genocide, since *The Diary of Anne Frank* is above all the story of a family behind closed doors. Although its author's tragic destiny contributes to the intensity of the story, it is primarily the story of family relations—notably Anne's relationship with her mother—and of Anne's awakening to love that fascinates young readers. In his work on personal diaries, Philippe Lejeune observes that the *Diary of Anne Frank* is what first inspires many people to write their own diaries.[30] And Bruno Bettelheim is quite harsh toward the Frank family. "The extraordinary world-wide success of the book, play, and movie *The Diary of Anne Frank* suggests the power of the desire to counteract the realization of the personality-destroying and murderous nature of the camps by concentrating all attention on what is experienced as a demonstration that private and intimate life can continue to flourish even under the direct persecution by the most ruthless totalitarian system. And this although Anne Frank's fate demonstrates how efforts at disregarding in private life what goes on around one in society can hasten one's own destruction." The worldwide success of Anne Frank's story, Bettelheim argues, "cannot be explained unless we recognize in it our wish to forget the gas chambers, and our effort to do so by glorifying the ability to retreat into an extremely private, gentle, sensitive world, and there to cling as much as possible to what have been one's usual daily attitudes and activities."[31] Bettelheim moves from a discussion of the success of the book to a consideration of the success of the film and the theatrical adaptation. He focuses on the ending of the film and theatrical versions, where one hears Anne's voice off camera or offstage: "In spite of everything, I still believe that people are really good at heart." Bettelheim comments: "This improbable sentiment is supposedly from a girl who had been starved to death, had watched her sister meet the same fate before she did, knew that her mother had been murdered, and had watched untold thousands of adults and children being killed. This statement is not justified by anything Anne actually told her diary."[32] What, then, is the function of this entirely fabricated final act of faith in the goodness of the human race? It is there to reassure—mistakenly, according to Bettelheim. It

> falsely reassures since it impresses on us that in the combat between Nazi terror and continuance of intimate family living the latter wins out, since Anne has the last word. This is simply contrary to fact, because it was she who got killed. Her seeming survival through her moving statement about the goodness of men releases us effectively of the need to cope with the problems Auschwitz presents. That is why we are so relieved by her statement. It explains why millions loved the play and movie, because while it confronts us with the fact that Auschwitz existed, it encourages us at the same time to ignore any of its implications. If all men are good at heart, there never really was an Auschwitz; nor is there any possibility that it may recur.[33]

Alvin Rosenfeld, studying the reception of *The Diary of Anne Frank* in the United States, observes that in the mid-1950s, Americans were not ready to confront the Holocaust. Are they more so today? There is reason for doubt. In the 1990s, Harry James Cargas, a U.S. academic and theologian, expressed his admiration for Anne Frank in terms that echoed the critics of the 1950s: "The compassionate child, never forgetting to go beyond herself, to see the miserable condition of others rather than to wallow in her own situation as many of us might have done, despite all, evinced hope. Each time I read the *Diary* I cannot help but feel that this time she'll make it, she'll survive."[34]

Thus optimism triumphs, as it triumphed in *Holocaust* and in *Schindler's List*. The history of the genocide, it seems, should not be end in despair. The story should be told in a way that saves the idea of man. It is this optimistic imperative that underwrites the tour of history offered at the Holocaust Memorial Museum in Washington:

> Visitors will learn that while this is overwhelmingly a story about the extermination of the Jewish people, it is also about the Nazis' plans for the annihilation of the Gypsies and the handicapped, and about the persecution of priests and patriots, Polish intellectuals and Soviet prisoners of war, homosexuals and even innocent children.
>
> Then, finally, when breaking hearts can bear it no longer, visitors will emerge into light—into a celebration of resistance, rebirth, and renewal for the survivors—whether they remained in Europe, or as so

many did, went to Israel or America to rebuild their lives. And having witnessed the nightmare of evil, the great American monuments to democracy that surround each departing visitor will take on a new meaning, as will the ideals for which they stand.[35]

The museum in Washington has already drawn crowds of visitors. It is a major instrument in the education of present and future generations. For Michael Berenbaum, it also aids in the "Americanization of the Holocaust," which manifests itself in the very goal the museum set for itself: it is addressed to Americans and should play a role in the political future of the United States. To do this, the museum should not address itself only to Jews. Instead, "The story had to be told in such a way that it would resonate not only with the survivor in New York and his children in San Francisco, but with a black leader from Atlanta, a Midwestern farmer, or a northeastern industrialist."[36] Berenbaum thus assigns a clear goal to the telling of the Holocaust story: to make reality comprehensible, to respond to the social needs of today's Americans.

Noemi Paiss, director of communications for the museum, explains the idea behind the memorial's mission in different terms. The goal of the museum, she told the *New York Times,* is an "en-masse understanding that we are not only about what the Germans did to Jews but what people did to people."[37]

The museum's link to the Steven Spielberg Foundation lies first in the fact that the same man, Michael Berenbaum, the promoter of the "Americanization of the Holocaust," assumed in succession the directorship of these two projects, equally monumental, equally

crowned with success and which, each in its own domain, relegate their predecessors to insignificance. The
first Memorial to the Martyrs of the Shoah on rue Geof-
froy-l'Asnier and Yad Vashem appear provincial next to
the memorial in Washington. The 130 interviews—perhaps 300 hours—collected by the French satellite of the
Fortunoff Archive seems paltry compared to the 1,700
hours taped in France by Steven Spielberg's teams,
which, moreover, reinterviewed certain survivors who
had already given their testimony for the Fortunoff
Archive. We can always console ourselves by affirming,
in this case, that the Fortunoff interviews are certainly
better, that they were conducted by persons with better
training, that their protocols better respect the personality of the witnesses, that their location at the National
Archives is prestigious, and that this inscribes these testimonies in national memory. But the fact is, we find
ourselves in the situation of a small grocer threatened
with disappearance by the superstores, or like a small
tailor competing with a large clothing manufacturer.
Above all, we must not hide from reality: with a few ex-
ceptions, the survivors of the deportation prefer the interviewing procedures used by Steven Spielberg's teams
to those of Yale. They like to show off their homes,
which they prepare specially for the interview. They are
happy to have their grandchildren join them at the end
of the interview. But above all, Steven Spielberg's fame
spills over onto them and gives them the impression that
they are basking in the light of his celebrity.

Testimony given spontaneously, and testimony solicited by the needs of justice, have given way to the social imperative of memory. The survivor was supposed to honor a "duty to remember," which, morally, he could not evade. Survivors had hoped for the chance to deliver their testimony ever since they left the camps. The act of bearing witness in front of the camera, of being able afterward to show the tape to their grandchildren, holds an essential importance for the survivors. "For many of us," Primo Levi observed, "being interviewed was a unique and memorable occasion, an event we had been waiting for since the day of the liberation and that even gave our liberation a meaning."[38] What difference does it make if this act could not take place until half a century later? For those who frequently feared they would not be believed, saying what life was like during the Holocaust validates an experience that, as many survivors have said and written, quickly began to seem unreal to them, often from the very moment of liberation.

The psychoanalyst Anne-Lise Stern, who was deported to Birkenau, observes that documents (notably those from which history is written) are made of paper. "Paper is also made from rags, from scraps, 'paper, rags, scrap iron for sale.' What are we? What am I? the survivor asks. All those who were deported in truth bear witness to that, to the scraps they have become. Knowledge of the deportation is that—knowledge of waste, of scraps. But when they speak of it, testify to it, they are no longer scraps."[39] Henri Borlant, deported at age fourteen in 1942, expresses the same thought in more ordinary terms: "Asleep within every former inmate is a humiliated being."[40] When former inmates know that they are at least being truly listened to, if not understood, testimony returns their dignity to them, in the very part of their identity that had been humiliated: that of former concentration camp inmates or ghetto survivors. In this sense, the recording of testimonies, when carried out with respect, responds to the desire that Robert Antelme expressed bluntly in a rarely read text that appeared in 1948. "The veritable hemorrhaging of expression—experienced by everyone, whether or not he was a writer—expresses one truth that encompasses all the others: namely, that each of us wants to put his entire effort into recognizing himself in that time now past and that each wants to make it understood that the man speaking now and the man who was over there are one and the same."[41] In this sense, it might seem that gathering testimonies is also a way of repairing the irreparable.

It is no coincidence that many involved in interviewing survivors have familial ties to this history. They are in search of a family story that history has denied them. Nathan Beyrak, director of the Israeli satellite of the Yale Archive, who also led the Ukrainian and Belarusian projects, writes: "I have no details of the murders of my relatives, my grandmother and her mother, sons, and daughter—my mother's two brothers and sister—which probably took place in the death pits near Slonim. I always felt compelled to know, to learn the most intimate details of what they experienced, moment by moment. I think the nearest I got to satisfying my curiosity was when I taped the testimony of a man who was taken to the very same death pits, possibly together with my family, and described the experience in great detail. Unlike my relatives, he fell into the pits without being hit by a bullet, and later managed to climb out."[42] Thus testimony reestablishes not only the identity of the survivors but also the identities of the descendants of those who died without graves, by allowing them to imagine the circumstances of their relatives' deaths and thus to begin the work of mourning.

The injunction to former inmates to testify, to tell their story to the young, to "package" their history so that their testimony can serve posthumously to educate future generations, also includes, however, an imperative that irritates certain of them. "Be Deported and Testify": that is the provocative title Anne-Lise Stern gave to her contribution to a recent colloquium. There is in this title a rejection of a double constraint: to be enclosed within a single identity, that of the inmate; and to be, as an inmate, nothing but one who testifies. Anne-Lise Stern is uncomfortable with being thus trapped in a set of demands greater than she, that causes her in some sense to lose her freedom, and whose ends are not unproblematic:

The pedagogy of memory, its necessity, can also have perverse effects. Survivors wish more and more to unburden themselves of their history, to unburden and soothe their close family, to universalize that history. Interviewers who may or may not be trained to listen, historians, sociologists, filmmakers, philosophers, or other intellectuals—they take up this task, or seize hold of it, by necessity and often with noble intentions. But then some start accusing the others of claiming a 'copyright' on Auschwitz. It could be that all sides, psychoanalysts among them, in fact dispossess the survivors and the dead. Will we become, all of us, nothing more or less than "ragpickers of History"?[43]

In place of the complaint of not being able to speak upon returning because no one listened, we now see another complaint, one that was already voiced after the broadcast of *Holocaust*: that of being all of a sudden dispossessed—but also exploited and reified in a competition among various specialists, a competition that undeniably is under way. Anne-Lise Stern approvingly cites the reflections of another former inmate, Henry Bulawko, who testified on his return from the camp and who has been the main organizer of associations of former Jewish inmates in France. "At a conference," he said, "I heard historians declare that former camp inmates were documents to them. . . . I expressed my surprise. They replied with a friendly smile: 'Living documents.' I suddenly saw myself transformed into a strange animal caged in a zoo with other rare species. Historians came to examine me, told me to lie down, turned me over and over as you turn the pages of a document, and asked me questions, taking notes here and there. . . . The term used at the conference seemed to me infinitely shocking. One can go from being a 'former inmate' to a 'witness,' then from 'witness' to 'document.' So then, what are we? What am I?"[44]

Although it would be possible simply to question the competence of the historian who dared speak to the witness in this way, Henry Bulawko is raising the problem of the tension between the witness and the historian, a tension, even a rivalry—and, why not say it outright, a power struggle—that is at the heart of current debates over the history of the contemporary era, but which is also found in other areas where individual expression comes into conflict with intellectual discourse. Philippe Lejeune, addressing defenders of canonical literature who denigrate autobiography, writes: "You act like a professional threatened by amateurs, or like certain professors I've met who have claimed their territory and don't appreciate it when someone challenges the legitimacy of their claim."[45] Lejeune adds: "There are those who know and those who heal. Bosses and nurses. Those who hold conferences and those who set to work in the workshop. Those who milk others' lives, those who churn them into theses, those who place them in archives. . . . Power cannot be avoided, but one can try to share it."[46]

When faced with the testimony of the inmates, historians find themselves in an impossible situation. It is the professional imperative of the historian, as Pierre Laborie reminds us, to be

a memory critic [un trouble-mémoire], careful not to forget that lines of division exist, that not all gaps can be closed: gaps between convictions born of lived experience and critical inquiries into the unfolding of the past coming from more distant sources; gaps between the virtues of commemoration and the rigor of the historical method; gaps between moments of amnesia or the reconstructed arrangement of time and the hard

realities of minutely reconstituted chronology; gaps
between the tricks played by retrospection and the
refusal to swim with the current so as to be able to
continue to observe men and events critically; gaps between memories that constitute identity, create solidarity, and form a "fraternity of a superior essence,"
and memories subjected to strict autopsies, examined
and cross-checked according to the demands of truth;
gaps between the seductive coherence of a discourse
that makes everything explicit, and the effort to track
down the unsaid, the forgotten, the silences; gaps between the legitimation that takes place when the past
is too perfectly reconstituted, and a legitimate effort
to preserve one's commitments, heritage, and values
from banalization.[47]

Although Pierre Laborie is speaking here of the Resistance, his analysis could apply equally to Holocaust testimonies. But can the historian, when face to face with
a living person, act morally as a "memory critic"? The
suffering conveyed by the story of a survivor—by one
who may be the last repository of a procession of the
dead whose memory he carries with him—paralyzes
the historian. The historian knows that all life stories
are constructions, but also that these (re)constructions
are the very armature, the vertebral column, of life in the
present. Historians find themselves faced with a problem that is almost impossible to resolve because two
moral imperatives come into conflict. Each person has
the right to fashion her own history, to put together
what she remembers or forgets in her own way. Sum-
marizing his life in his only book, written in the twilight

of his life, Marcel Lévy observes: "Because our ideas today are not those of our adolescence, because our ruined body offers only a vague resemblance to the one we inhabited forty years ago, memory alone remains to affirm the continuity of our being. Our life, or what is left of it, is suspended from those few beads of the rosary strung on the subtle cord of memory, which we always fear will break. And still, what guarantees do we have that those remnants of memory are really firsthand?"[48] Each person has an absolute right to her memory, which is nothing other than her identity, her very being. But this right can come into conflict with an imperative of the historian's profession, the imperative of an obstinate quest for the truth.

Some, like Lucy Dawidowicz and Raul Hilberg, prefer to distance themselves from testimonies, never subjecting them to critique, ignoring them altogether, or abandoning them to oblivion or to other disciplines such as literary criticism or psychology that do not maintain the same relationship to truth. Alternatively, historians can read, listen to, and watch testimonies without looking for what they know is not to be found—clarification of precise events, places, dates, and numbers, which are wrong with the regularity of a metronome—but knowing also that testimony contains extraordinary riches: an encounter with the voice of someone who has lived through a piece of history; and, in oblique fashion, not factual truth, but the more subtle and just as indispensable truth of an epoch and of an experience.

The conflicts we sometimes see between witnesses and historians probably stem to a large extent from the recent blurring of boundaries between the areas for which each is responsible and between the roles each is assigned. Witnesses and historians are summoned to the same places: the witness stand, radio and television studios, classrooms. They often find themselves cast as rivals. The "duty to remember" calls for much more from witnesses and their testimony than an account of a lived experience. For instance, the explicit goal of the Survivors of the Shoah Visual History Foundation is ambitious: "The archive will be used as a tool for global education about the Holocaust and to teach racial, ethnic and cultural tolerance. By preserving the eyewitness testimonies of tens of thousands of Holocaust survivors, the Foundation will enable future generations to learn the lessons of this devastating period in human history from those who survived."[49] The goal, then, is quite simply to replace teachers with witnesses, who are supposed to be bearers of a knowledge that, sadly enough, they possess no more than anyone else. Primo Levi, who reflected deeply on this question and who delivered his testimony not only in his writings but also in a large number of classrooms, expressed his exhaustion and skepticism toward the end of this life:

> One of the questions that gets repeated and repeated is the question of why it happened, why there are wars, why the camps were built, why the Jews were exterminated, and it is a question to which I have no

answer. No one does. Why there are wars, why there was the First World War and the Second World War and now we talk all the time of a Third World War, is a question that torments me because I have no answer. My standard reply is that it is part of our animal make-up, that a sense, an awareness of territory is something we share with dogs, nightingales, all animals; but even as I say it, I don't believe it. . . . Well, I have only vague, generic answers, that man is evil, man is not good. And there is another question I am constantly asked: is man good? How can anyone answer such a question? There are good people and less good people, each of us is a mixture of good and not so good.[50]

Primo Levi stopped going to classrooms to give his testimony because his experience as a concentration camp inmate did not provide him with answers to any of the questions asked of him. But not all the witnesses are as rigorous and demanding as Primo Levi; the fact that they are survivors does not make then any less men and women, complete with human vanity. How can anyone resist giving a history lesson, especially to the young? How can they find the courage to say that the concentration camp experience does not confer any prophetic talent, that, sadly, it does not permit any better understanding of how to fight future barbarism? Most often, the witnesses depart from their role, explain to the students the rise of Nazism and its multiple crimes, and attempt to mobilize them for the battles of the moment. The witnesses perform this task, moreover, largely with the consent of teachers, who thus evade the dry task of teaching the history of the Holocaust. Some teachers pre-

fer not to teach the subject, replacing lessons with a film
or a discussion with a witness, whereas pedagogy demands that history lessons and the witness's testimony
both be presented, which did not happen, for instance,
at the forum following the broadcast of *Holocaust* on
French television, from which both historians and teachers of history were absent.

What is there to testify about, then? What knowledge
do the survivors possess—because they must certainly
possess some knowledge? What does the audience expect from testimony? Is a story of atrocity supposed to
inoculate us against future atrocity? Anne-Lise Stern
asks herself these questions: "We are expected, we are
urged to testify 'before it is too late.' Yet, what knowledge do they hope to gain? What deathbed confession,
what family secret, do they expect to hear? Where is all
this listening to survivors leading, whether by those who
have had little education about the Holocaust or by
those who are overeducated? Toward sound bites, I fear,
which future generations will play with and enjoy. It's
happening already."

And she adds: "For the teaching of horror always
threatens to become itself a source of pleasure. To the
three impossible professions mentioned by Freud—education, government, and psychoanalysis—must one now
add a fourth: bearing witness?"[51] Perhaps she is right.

□ □ □

Testimony, then, has changed. Survivors are no longer
motivated to tell their stories before the camera purely

by an internal necessity, though this necessity still exists. A veritable social imperative now transforms the witness into an apostle and prophet. The decline of communism at the end of the 1980s has also made travel to the sites of the annihilation of the Jews—Auschwitz-Birkenau most importantly—easy and relatively inexpensive. Young people from every country visit in greater and greater numbers, accompanied by former camp inmates. Knowledge will thus come from a confrontation with the real, the "true": the reality of the site, the reality of the former inmate's "experience." The objective of such undertakings corresponds to another stereotype that is becoming increasingly common, namely, the transformation of the young, those of the third generation after the events, into "witnesses for the witness," bearers of a knowledge of the destruction of the Jews acquired not at school, for instance, or from books, but from a lived experience. This model seems to recall the Gospels: these young people will be the apostles who, once the witnesses have disappeared, will be able to carry on their word. But what word? What do witnesses speak of? Of what they remember, and only this memory has the force of the real. Nathan Beyrak reports a strange interview with a man who had been part of a group of children who, having survived in the Kovno ghetto until its evacuation in 1944, were sent to various camps in Poland and Germany, including Birkenau and Mauthausen. The man Beyrak discusses came for a first testimony session. He spoke for three hours, telling a story Beyrak describes as "dry." Returning home, he suddenly remembered that he had a series of

notes there, a sort of ghetto diary whose existence he
had forgotten. He dug out the diary and discovered that
it mentioned many things he had not covered in his testimony. He had to testify again. At the next session, he
came equipped with his diary and told new stories, reading extracts from the diary before the camera. But the
person conducting the interview noticed that he was
skipping over certain pages in the diary and she asked
why. He replied that certain things written in the journal could not possibly have taken place, because he had
no memory of them whatsoever. Nevertheless, when
one reads these pages, particularly the description of
hunger, there can be no doubt about their authenticity.
But the witness did not want to read these pages aloud.
They seemed to him simply "unreal." As Beyrak notes,
he simply could not connect his memories with the experience described in the diary.[52]

If the testimony of this witness had been recorded
shortly after the end of the war, his story would have
been different from the one Beyrak recorded some fifty
years later. Every testimony is recorded at a precise moment in time, and as such may be instrumentalized in
political and ideological contexts that, like all such contexts, are bound to change. The moment when a testimony is delivered tells us a great deal about the society
in which the witness lives. Today, for example, survivors
of the French deportation tend to tell similar stories.
They were deported by Vichy, poorly received in France
after their return, and no one helped them reintegrate
into society. They did not, for instance, receive help from
psychologists or specialized educators. But this version

of events overlooks the fact that psychology did not have the same status in 1945 as it has today and that even the profession of educator was still in its infancy. This is a discourse of resentment toward France, which disregards Nazi Germany. The "Boche" or the "Teuton," a figure that was common in stories from the immediate postwar years, has disappeared. Witnesses no longer tell, as they once did, how they kissed the ground of France on their return or cried with emotion on hearing "La Marseillaise." Witnesses always give their stories goals beyond the scope of the particular story. These goals change over time. In the postwar years, the dominant idea was that Germany—an "intrinsically" barbaric Germany—had to be stopped from coming back to life.[53] Today, all the witnesses, in France and elsewhere, cite as their goal the fight against Holocaust denial and the resurgence of "fascism." In addition, there is sometimes the fight against the "genocides" that continue to take place in various countries. This discourse, which has become stereotypical, is embedded in the surrounding political discourse, which is, as it were, superimposed on the testimonies that it in turn instrumentalizes.

The discourse of the witnesses is also determined by their age. The witnesses of the 1990s, those who testified during the explosion of testimony, were for the most part men and women of retirement age who will have no more children. For these witnesses, as for everyone in old age, the future and the possibilities it opens have shrunk vastly. The tone of their testimonies is heavily influenced by the ways they think about and assess their lives. A witness may have the sense of having succeeded in life, or of having failed, with, of course, a whole range of positions in between. The interview, however, is taking place because of the person's experience during World War II, even if he or she is asked to discuss the periods before and after the war as well. Witnesses are being interviewed as "survivors" or "former inmates." What is collected, therefore, is not a "life story" but rather—and this is clear to both interviewers and witnesses—the story of the witness's life (before and after, but above all during) as it is informed by the time of the war, a time that is therefore postulated to mark a fundamental rupture. The very notion of a "before" leads to anachronisms or teleology. "After" indicates that the interviewer is asking the witness to consider this event as a moment of origin. Elie Wiesel referred to Auschwitz as a new Sinai, the place of a new covenant. In psychoanalytic terms, the Holocaust has become a new primal scene. We are therefore in the presence of a second myth of origins. An individual's entire history thus finds itself knotted around the years of life spent in the camp or the ghettos because of a pure postulate: that that experience was the decisive experience of his or her life. This, however, remains to be proven, something no one has yet undertaken. Ruth Klüger is, to my knowledge, the only one to have protested against this image of the former inmate. "And yet in the eyes of many, Auschwitz is a point of origin for survivors. The name itself has an aura, albeit a negative one, that came with the patina of time, and people who want to say something important about me announce that I have been in Auschwitz. But whatever you may think, I don't hail from Auschwitz, I come from Vienna. Vienna is a part of me—that's where I acquired consciousness and acquired language—but Auschwitz was as foreign to me as the moon. Vienna is part of my mind-set, while Auschwitz was a lunatic terra incognita, the memory of which is like a bullet lodged in the soul where no surgery can reach it. Auschwitz was merely a gruesome accident."[54]

Others have perhaps protested through their silence. In certain refusals to testify, might there not be something other than the fear of awakening memories that are too painful, namely, the fear of being trapped in an image in which one does not quite recognize oneself?

□ □ □

How can the explosion of testimony be explained? What drives this collection of video testimonies, which demands so much time and money? For some, at issue is the creation of an oral history archive in the traditional sense. The collection at the Holocaust Memorial Museum in Washington is thus called an oral history archive. For others, these testimony projects are a desperate effort to rescue the individual from the masses, to give voice to ordinary people who have neither the desire nor perhaps the ability to put their stories in writing. The same motivations are at work in this case and in the memorial books. Whereas theology and sociology speak of the "Holocaust," explains Aharon Appelfeld, himself a survivor of the genocide, "Literature says: 'let's take a look at this particular person. Let's give him a name. Let's give him a place; put a cup of coffee in his hand'. . . . The strength of literature lies in its ability to convey intimacy . . . the kind of intimacy that touches your own."[55] Nathan Beyrak, who directs the Israeli satellite of the Fortunoff Archive, in a text entitled "To Rescue the Individual Out of the Mass Number: Intimacy as a Central Concept in Oral History," affirms that the concept of intimacy is the central theme of research in his group.

Two aspects of the video testimony collections stand out, then. The first is a constant throughout the Jewish memory of the Holocaust: to return a name, a face, a history to each of the victims of mass murder. This was the project of the memorial books. It was Serge Klarsfeld's project when he published *Memorial to the Jews Deported from France* in 1978, a work containing the names and vital statistics of all the adult Jews deported from France, and when he published *Memorial to the Jewish Children Deported from France* in 1994, which also included photos of the deported children. It was also in the name of the dead, of each of the dead, that Gideon Hausner spoke in presenting the charges against Adolf Eichmann: "As I stand here before you, Judges of Israel, to lead the prosecution of Adolf Eichmann, I do not stand alone. With me, in this place and at this hour, stand six million accusers. But they cannot rise to their feet and point an accusing finger toward the man who sits in the glass dock and cry: 'I accuse!' . . . Therefore it falls on me to be their spokesman."[56] In the memorial books, in Serge Klarsfeld's books, and in Hausner's words, however, what is at issue is the name and memory of the dead. In the video archives, at issue are the

living, the survivors. The concept of intimacy evoked by
Nathan Beyrak applies to them. This concept lies at the
heart of the current movement to collect testimonies and
the frequent appearances of witnesses on radio and television programs. But this concept of intimacy is not confined to Holocaust testimony. Instead, it is at the heart
of how our society and our media function. The sociologist Dominique Mehl observes that this concept signals
"a crisis of expert discourse and a calling into question
of the pedagogical authority of the learned and of specialists"[57]—including, of course, historians. The television of intimacy, evident in a large number of programs,
is based on "the expression of emotions and on testimonies." It puts experience on display and it privileges
showing.[58] The filming technique, moreover, is the same
in television broadcasts and in the recording of survivor
testimony; in both, the close-up is favored. "Moreover,
the director is on the lookout for body language that
may betray feelings or emotions. Looks, gestures, hands,
are so many offerings to the technicians. In the programs of intimacy, the eye of the camera tracks the eye
of the witness."[59] Such programs allow the one who testifies to "perfect his social identity," the identity that requires the other's gaze, even society's approval, since
there are times when a way of being requires socializa-
tion in order to become truly constitutive of personality
or singularity. "Otherwise, it risks becoming a stigma or
a curious eccentricity," Mehl suggests. "Recognition by
the collectivity authorizes one to accept oneself and to
demand that others assist in the constitution of identity.
A certain degree of visibility is necessary to give defini-

tion to one's personality and to one's place in the world." This affirmation of identity through witnessing, however, produces a problem when the testimony concerns not only an individual trauma (a rape, for example) but also suffering born of a historical event. The historical event becomes fragmented into a series of individual stories. We are thus confronted, as Richard Sennett observes, with "an ideology of intimacy: social relationships of all kinds are real, believable, and authentic the closer they approach the inner psychological concerns of each person. This ideology transmutes political categories into psychological categories."[60]

Testimony appeals to the heart and not to the mind. It elicits compassion, pity, indignation, even rebellion. The one who testifies signs a "compassionate pact" with the one who receives the testimony, just as someone who writes an autobiography signs what Philippe Lejeune calls an "autobiographical pact" with the reader.[61] Dominique Mehl characterizes this pact as a "specific interaction between transmission and reception. On the side of the transmission, the compassionate protocol requires placing the exhibition of the individual and his particular suffering at the center of the enterprise, and emphasizes emotional displays and bodily expression. On the side of reception, identification with the victims and empathy with the sufferers constitute the springboard for compassionate response."[62] In this light, Nazism and the Holocaust enter the public sphere principally because they devastated the lives of individuals who triumphed over death, even if many today affirm that they have never left Auschwitz.

This vision troubles historians. This is not because historians are insensitive to suffering, or because they themselves are not overwhelmed by these stories of pain and fascinated by some of them. Rather, this uneasiness stems from the sense that this juxtaposition of stories is not a historical narrative, and that, in some sense, it annuls historical narrative. For how can a coherent historical discourse be constructed if it is constantly countered by another truth, the truth of individual memory? How can the historian incite reflection, thought, and rigor when feelings and emotions invade the public sphere?

EPILOGUE

THE PAPON TRIAL, OR THE DELEGATION OF WITNESSING

The Eichmann trial marked the advent of the witness. The Papon trial marked a double delegation of witnessing. The role of the witness was delegated first to the historians, who became witnesses for the prosecution, the defense, or the plaintiff. Everything there is to be said about this confusion of roles was said during the trial and in the works published immediately after the trial. But also—and this is what really interests me here—the Papon trial marked the delegation of witnessing to a new generation, that of the children who grew up during the war and for whom the memory of a traumatic past no longer resides in the recollection of particular events, about which nothing can be said, but in the irremediable shock those events created in their young lives.

Every trial has one or several testimonies that seem to carry more weight than the others, that make a stronger impression both on those participating in the trial and on the audience following the trial as it is reported in the media. In the Papon trial, there was general agreement that Esther Fogiel gave one such testimony. "It would be indecent to rank the testimonies of the victims," remarks Eric Conan, "but Esther Fogiel's testimony mesmerized the audience."

Esther Fogiel took the stand on the thirty-seventh day of the trial, December 19, 1997. Prior to her appearance, the court had heard other witnesses whose relatives had been taken from Bordeaux to Drancy and Auschwitz. Even at age seventy, Georges Gheldmann uttered the same words he had used as a child to explain how "someone had taken mommy away." Éliane Dommange, who was eight years old when her parents were deported, recalled waiting in vain for their return. But the tragedy seemed to be even more relentless for Ester Fogiel, "a sparrow's silhouette . . . relating her tragedies in a little girl's voice, with the images and impressions of a child,"[1] "a small triangular face that seemed to be from before the war."[2]

What story did Esther Fogiel tell? She told first of her childhood as the daughter of immigrants, whose parents had arrived in France in the 1920s "to flee the pogroms" of their native Latvia. Little did it matter that there were few pogroms in Latvia in the 1920s, that the massive immigration of the years following World War I were essentially the result of a disastrous economic situation. Collective memory prefers the idea that the wave of migration in the 1920s was a flight from anti-Semitism. Like all immigrants, Esther Fogiel's parents worked hard. Her mother transferred her from one nanny to another from the age of six months. It was only when her

father, who had enlisted in the French army, was demo-
bilized in 1940, that her parents brought her back home.
No longer able to manage his own business, her father
became a dockworker. They then left for the unoccupied
zone. One day, her mother picked her up at school and
took her to the home of a young couple. "She looked at
me with a sad smile that impressed me deeply." Left
with a woman she did not know, Esther Fogiel found
herself in Valence-d'Agen with a family whose behavior
toward her changed abruptly three days after her arrival. They became brutal. Later, she came to think that
they changed their attitude because they had learned
that her parents had been deported and that they would
not receive the stipulated payments. She was raped, then
spent time in a religious institution, where she was kept
isolated from others and treated "like the devil's helper."
Afterward, she returned to the foster family, where she
was forced to perform the most awful chores. The foster family was in fact a threesome, composed of the
wife, her husband, and her lover. Frequently, she was
made to sleep in the husband's bed. Her only tie of af-
fection was to a small dog. One night she heard its
groans and, at daybreak, found the dog hanging above
her bed. "I see it still," she stated. In 1945, her foster
parents were arrested and imprisoned. She never tried
to find out why. Returning to her neighborhood after
the war, she recognized a dress of her mother's being
worn by a stranger. "All my life," she added, "I have
never stopped making the journey to Auschwitz." At
age thirty, she recalled on the stand, she attempted
suicide.

Éric Conan and Bertrand Poirot-Delpech, two observers of the trial whose analyses quite often disagree, share a common appreciation of Esther Fogiel's testimony. "Seeing this shadow knocked around by life, and recalling the arguments against the trial, I told myself that if the trial managed to console Esther Fogiel even a little, it would not be in vain, and that this outcome for a single one of the victims sufficed to justify the trial, to make it a sacred duty," writes Poirot-Delpech.[3] And Éric Conan, who does not refrain from criticizing the trial, notes, precisely with reference to Esther Fogiel's testimony, that for all the witnesses "the judicial inquiry constitutes the least refutable of the arguments advanced in favor of the Papon trial. This 'trial for history' does not serve history. This 'trial for national memory' breeds confusion. But, depending on the final verdict, it does answer to the victims' need to find the origin of their pain."[4]

Esther Fogiel is certainly an extreme case. Other children separated from their parents were fortunate to be welcomed into warmer environments. But her sufferings, even her suicide attempt, are echoed to varying degrees in the experience of many who, as children, had to be hidden to escape persecution and who today are beginning to express themselves, notably in the newsletters of the hidden children associations that have been formed in France, the United States, Israel, Poland, and elsewhere. Esther Fogiel's testimony seems to be echoed in books such as Berthe Burko-Falcman's poignant novel, L'enfant caché [The hidden child].[5] While Holocaust survivor associations have seen their numbers dwindle drastically and worry about their future, associations of members of the second generation are flourishing.

Testimony thus detaches itself from history, distances itself farther from the event, somewhat the way waves of an earthquake spread out from its epicenter. Reading or hearing the voices of these "hidden children," one learns much about childhood and about humanity, about the violence inflicted by certain traumas and their irreparable character. But does one learn history? The repercussions of an event inform us about the power of that event but do not account for what the event was.

The third generation after the war is being born. The "hidden children," within whom the murdered child continues to live, are becoming grandparents in their turn, even as they relive their memories of the war.

What, then, is the duty of historians, of those who produce historical narratives? What is the duty of history teachers, who introduce the young to this story? Should they, as sometimes happens today, wage war against memory and against the witnesses, battling them for control of editorial space, media coverage, and organizational power—at the risk of expending a large amount of their energy on this battle? I do not believe so. Historians have but one obligation, to follow their profession, even if the results of their labors fuel public debate or collective memory, even if they are instrumentalized by political agents. Because when traces fade with time, what remains is the written record of events in history, which is the only future of the past.

NOTES

Introduction

1. Quoted by Pierre Vidal-Naquet in "Simon Doubnov: L'homme moderne," preface to *Histoire moderne du peuple juif,* by Simon Doubnov, trans. Samuel Jankélévitch (Paris: Le Cerf, 1994), v.

2. During a visit to the institute in 1993, I ascertained that these testimonies had not yet been catalogued. Since then, a team of researchers under the supervision of Professor Feliks Tych has prepared the entirety of these archives for publication, along with a critical apparatus. The first volume, prepared under the supervision of one of the foremost experts in the history of the Warsaw ghetto, Ruta Sakowska, was published in 1998. The second and third volumes appeared in 2000 and 2002 respectively: *Relacje z Zagłady. Inwentarz* [Holocaust survivor testimonies], Record Group 301, ed. Jewish Historical Archives (Warsaw: Jewish Historical Institute [ZIH], Instytut Naukowo-Badawczy), vol. 1 (1–900), vol. 2 (901–2000), vol. 3 (2001–3000).

3. This information is drawn from the memoirs of the historian Lucy S. Dawidowicz, *From that Place and Time: A*

Memoir: 1938–1947 (New York: W.W. Norton, 1989), 304ff.

4. Raul Hilberg, "I Was Not There," in *Writing and the Holocaust,* ed. Berel Lang (New York: Holmes & Meier, 1988), 18.

5. Philip Friedman and Jacob Robinson, *Guide to Jewish History under Nazi Impact* (New York: Yivo Institute for Jewish Research, 1960); Philip Friedman, *Bibliography of Books in Hebrew on the Jewish Catastrophe and Heroism in Europe* (New York: Yivo Institute for Jewish Research, 1960); and Philip Friedman and Joseph Gar, *Bibliography of Yiddish Books on the Catastrophe and Heroism* (New York, 1962).

6. TN: Because the word "Holocaust" means "burnt sacrifice," French scholars prefer "Shoah," taken from the title of Claude Lanzmann's film. The translation follows common U.S. usage in employing the term "Holocaust."

7. Marc Bloch, *Écrits de guerre 1914–1918,* ed. Étienne Bloch (Paris: Armand Colin, 1997), 170.

8. Lucy S. Dawidowicz, *The Holocaust and the Historians* (Cambridge, Mass.: Harvard University Press, 1981), 177.

9. I have already broached this subject in the second part of *Déportation et génocide: Entre la mémoire et l'oubli* (Paris: Plon, 1992; repr. Hachette-Pluriel, 1995).

I. Witnesses to a Drowning World

1. Quoted in Jacob Sloan, introduction to Emmanuel Ringelblum, *Notes from the Warsaw Ghetto: The Journal of Emmanuel Ringelblum,* ed. and trans. Jacob Sloan (New York: McGraw-Hill, 1958), xxi–xxii.

2. With Meier Balaban, Ignacy (Itzhak) Schiper (1884–1943) was one of the two main specialists in independent Poland on the history of the Jews.

3. Alexander Donat, *The Holocaust Kingdom* (New York: Holt Rinehart and Winston, 1963), 211.

4. Heinrich Himmler, *Geheimreden 1933 bis 1945 und andere Ansprachen,* ed. Bradley F. Smith and Agnes F. Peterson (Frankfurt/Main: Propyläen Verlag, 1974), 169–71.

5. Quoted in Tom Segev, *The Seventh Million: The Israelis and the Holocaust,* trans. Haim Watzman (New York: Henry Holt, 1991), 151.

6. Donat, *Holocaust Kingdom,* 211. Quoted in Rachel Ertel, *Dans la langue de personne: Poésie Yiddish de l'anéantissement* (Paris: Seuil, 1993), 23. Donat's work appeared in French under the title *Veilleur où est la nuit?* translated from the English by Claude Durand, preface by Elie Wiesel (Paris: Seuil, 1967).

7. David Bergelson, quoted in Richard Marienstras, *Être un peuple en diaspora* (Paris: François Maspero, 1975), 141.

8. No general history of the World War II ghettos exists in French, nor are there any scholarly monographs on any particular ghetto.

9. Raya Cohen, "Emmanuel Ringelblum: Between Historiographical Tradition and Unprecedented History," in *Gal-Ed: On the History of the Jews in Poland,* vols. 15–16 (Tel Aviv: Center for Research on the History of Polish Jewry, Diaspora Research Institute, Tel Aviv University, Graphit Press, 1997), 105–17.

10. Michel Borwicz, *Écrits des condamnés à mort sous l'occupation nazie* (Paris: Idées/Gallimard, 1973), 122.

11. *Relacje z Zaglady. Inwentarz.*

12. I am indebted here to the work of the historian Lucjan Dobroszycki, and particularly his introduction to *The Chronicle of Łódź Ghetto: 1941–1944,* ed. Lucjan Dobroszycki (New Haven: Yale University Press, 1984). In addition to a translation of the ghetto chronicle, the editor includes a collection of narratives and stories.

13. Quoted in Dobroszycki, introduction to *Chronicle of the Łódź Ghetto,* x.

14. Ibid., xn.7.

15. See Dobroszyski, *Chronicle of the Łódź Ghetto;* and

Łódź Ghetto: Inside a Community under Siege, ed. Alan Edelson and Robert Lapides (New York: Penguin Books, 1989).

16. Marc Bloch's "Réflexions d'un historien sur les fausses nouvelles de la guerre" was first published in *La Revue de Synthèse Historique* (1921). I have used the remarkable edition of the above-cited *Écrits de guerre,* 182.

17. Jurek Becker, *Jacob the Liar* (1969), trans. Leila Vennewitz (New York: Arcade Publishing, 1990), 7. I am grateful to Karla Grierson for calling my attention to this work.

18. Ibid., 60.

19. Bloch, *Écrits de guerre,* 182.

20. Borwicz, *Écrits des condamnés de mort,* 50.

21. Ringelblum, *Notes from the Warsaw Ghetto.*

22. Borwicz, *Écrits des condamnés de mort,* 49. This sociological study was a doctoral thesis, defended in 1952 at the Sorbonne before a jury composed of Professors Renouvin, Gurvitch, and Fabre. The 1973 Gallimard edition is augmented by the author.

23. Ibid., 48, author's italics.

24. Simha Guterman, *Le livre retrouvé,* ed. Nicole Lapierre, translated from the Yiddish [into French] by Aby Wieviorka (Paris: Plon, 1991), 15.

25. *The Warsaw Diary of Adam Czerniakow,* ed. and trans. Raul Hilberg, Stanislas Staron, and Josef Kermisz (New York: Stein and Day, 1982).

26. Calel Perechodnik, *Am I a Murderer?: Testament of a Jewish Ghetto Policeman,* ed. and trans. Frank Fox (Boulder. Colo.: Westview Press), 1996.

27. Primo Levi, *The Drowned and the Saved,* trans. Raymond Rosenthal (New York: Vintage, 1989), 18.

28. Nathan Beyrak, "To Rescue the Individual Out of the Mass Number: Intimacy as a Central Concept in Oral History," in *Ces visages qui nous parlent/These Faces Talk to Us,* ed. Maurice Cling and Yannis Thanassekos, Actes de rencontre audiovisuelle internationale sur le témoignage des survivants des camps de concentration et d'extermination Nazis

(Brussels: Fondation Auschwitz and Fondation pour la Mémoire de la Déportation, 1995), 141.

29. In Claude Lanzmann, *Shoah: The Complete Text of
the Acclaimed Holocaust Film,* preface by Simone de Beau-
voir (New York: Da Capo Press, 1995), 163–64.

30. Ibid., 164.

31. Raul Hilberg, "The Diary of Adam Czerniakow," in
*The Politics of Memory: The Journey of a Holocaust Histo-
rian* (Chicago: Ivan R. Dee, 1996), 176–88, 187, 185. Information and citations in what follows are from this essay.

32. Ibid., 185–86.

33. Ibid.,186.

34. Ibid., 188.

35. Richard Marienstras, *Diasporiques* no. 1 (1997): 5.

36. Chaim Kaplan, *The Warsaw Diary of Chaim Kaplan,*
ed. and trans. Abraham I. Katsch (New York: Collier, 1973);
Abraham Lewin, *Cup of Tears: A Diary of the Warsaw
Ghetto,* ed. Antony Polonsky, trans. Chris Hutton (Oxford:
Basil Blackwell, 1988); *Warsaw Ghetto: A Diary by Mary
Berg,* ed. S. L. Shneiderman (New York: L. B. Fischer, 1945);
Janusz Korczak, *Ghetto Diary* (New York: Holocaust Li-
brary, 1978). A new edition of Korczak's *Ghetto Diary,* in-
cluding letters and unedited documents, was translated into
French by Zofia Bobwicz (Paris: Robert Laffont, 1998).

37. These texts can be found in Bernard Mark, *Des voix
dans la nuit: La résistance juive à Auschwitz-Birkenau* (Paris:
Plon, 1982). English translations are found in *Amidst a
Nightmare of Crime,* ed. Jadwiga Bezwinska and Danuta
Czech (New York: Fertig, 1992).

38. Nicole Lapierre in Guterman, *Le livre retrouvé,* 19.

39. Perechodnik, *Am I a Murderer?* 191–92.

40. Ertel, *Dans la langue de personne,* 28.

41. On memorial books, see Annette Wieviorka and
Itzhok Niborski, *Les livres du souvenir: Mémoriaux juifs de
Pologne* (Paris: Archives-Gallimard, 1983); and *From a Ruined Garden: The Memorial Books of Polish Jewry,* ed. and
trans. Jack Kugelmass and Jonathan Boyarin (New York:

Schocken, 1983). This work contains a bibliography of memorial books which was exhaustive at the time of publication, compiled by Zachary M. Baker.

42. Marienstras, *Diasporiques,* 11.

43. Edgar Morin, *L'homme et la mort* (Paris: Seuil, 1976), 44.

44. Alain Finkielkraut, *The Imaginary Jew,* trans. Kevin O'Neill and David Suchoff (Lincoln: University of Nebraska Press, 1994). Also relevant are Henri Raczymow, *Contes d'exil et d'oubli* (Paris: Gallimard, 1979); "Fin du people ashkénaze?" in *Mille ans de cultures ashkénazes,* ed. Jean Baumgarten, Rachel Ertel, Itzhok Niborski, and Annette Wieviorka (Paris: Liana Levi, 1994); and Nicole Lapierre, *Le silence de la mémoire: À la recherche des Juifs de Plock* (Paris: Plon, 1989).

45. Abraham (Avrom) Sutzkever, born in 1913, was interned in the Vilna ghetto (see his testimony, "The Ghetto of Vilna," in *Le livre noir,* compiled by Ilya Ehrenbourg and Vassili Grossman, [Arles: Solin-Actes Sud, 1995], 499–590), escaped, joined the resistance, and fled to Moscow. He left the USSR in 1946 and settled in Israel in 1948. One of his volumes has been translated into French as *Où gîtent les étoiles* (Paris: Seuil, 1988).

46. Avrom Sutzkever, "Mon témoignage au procès de Nuremberg," translated from the Yiddish into French by Gilles Rozier, *Europe,* special issue, "Les écrivains de la guerre," (August–Sept. 1995): 140–53. Sutzkever's notes are reproduced as they were written, except for some syntactical corrections. I thank Gilles Rozier for calling my attention to this text.

47. "Witness," in Xavier Léon-Dufour, *Dictionary of the New Testament,* trans. Terrence Prendergast (San Francisco: Harper & Row, 1980), 431.

48. Rachel Ertel, "Écrit en yiddish," in *Autour d'Elie Wiesel,* ed. Michael de Saint-Chéron (Paris: Odile Jacob, 1996), 24.

49. The bibliography on Elie Wiesel is enormous. Until

recently, however, probably out of ignorance of Yiddish, no one thought to analyze comparatively Wiesel's first testimony in Yiddish and the retelling of the same story in French. Two articles, both appearing at the same time, have since undertaken this analysis: Rachel Ertel, "Écrit en yiddish"; and Naomi Seidman, "Elie Wiesel and the Scandal of Jewish Rage," *Jewish Social Studies* 3, no. 1 (Fall 1996): 1–19.

50. Jonas Turkow, *C'était ainsi, 1939–1943: La vie de ghetto de Varsovie,* translated from the Yiddish [into French] by Maurice Pfeffer (Paris: Austral, 1995). In Yiddish: *Azoi iz es geven* (Buenos Aires: Tsentral-farband fun Poylishe Yidn in Argentine, 1948).

51. Elie Wiesel, *Night,* trans. Stella Rodway (New York: Bantam, 1982), 1.

52. Quoted in Seidman, "Elie Wiesel," 5.

53. Wiesel, *Night,* iv.

54. Ibid., 109.

55. The beginning of this passage is translated in Seidman, "Elie Wiesel," 6–7.

56. The rest of the passage was translated into French by Wiesel himself in the first volume of his memoirs, *Tous les fleuves vont à la mer: Mémoires* (Paris: Seuil, 1994), 413. The translation reproduced here is from the English translation of Wiesel's memoirs, *All Rivers Run to the Sea: Memoirs* (New York: Schocken, 1995), 319–20, ellipses in original.

57. Wiesel, *Night,* 109.

58. Antoine Prost, *Douze leçons sur l'histoire* (Paris: Seuil, 1996), 249.

59. Seidman, "Elie Wiesel," 8.

60. François Mauriac, foreword to Wiesel, *Night,* ix.

61. On the theme of silence, see, among others, André Neher, "Le silence et l'être: Elie Wiesel," in *Exil de la parole: Du silence biblique au silence d'Auschwitz* (Paris: Éditions du Seuil, 1970), 228–45; and Myriam B. Cohen, *Elie Wiesel: Variations sur le silence* (La Rochelle: Rumeur des âges, 1988).

62. Wiesel, *Night,* 32.

63. See my *Déportation et génocide*.

64. On this point, see Wiesel, *All Rivers Run to the Sea,* 319ff.

65. Quoted in Ellen S. Fine, *Legacy of Night: The Literary Universe of Elie Wiesel* (Albany: SUNY Press, 1982), 30.

66. Notably David G. Roskies, *Against the Apocalypse: Responses to Catastrophe in Modern Jewish Culture* (Cambridge, Mass.: Harvard University Press, 1984); and Ertel, *Dans la langue de personne.*

67. Ertel, *Dans la langue de personne,* 42.

68. Alexandre Luria, *L'homme dont le monde volait en éclats* (Paris: Seuil, 1995).

69. I examine another example of this phenomenon below, 136–137.

70. Elie Wiesel, "Rand Makhhovès vegn yiddish" [Reflections on Yiddish–at the Edge, the Border, the Extremity] in *Di Goldene Keyt,* no. 123 (1987): 26. Quoted in Ertel, "Écrit en Yiddish," 23, translated into French by Ertel.

71. Ertel, "Écrit en Yiddish," 27.

72. Giovanni Tesio, quoted in *Primo Levi: Tragedy of an Optimist,* by Myrian Anissimow, trans. Steven Cox (Woodstock, N.Y.: Overlook Press, 1999), 329.

73. Rochelle G. Saidel, *Never Too Late to Remember: The Politics behind New York City's Holocaust Museum* (New York: Holmes & Meier, 1996).

74. Ibid., 48.

75. On these questions, see my *Déportation et génocide*.

76. See Hilberg's autobiography, *The Politics of Memory.*

77. Saidel, "Elie Wiesel," 3.

78. See Annette Wieviorka, "Un lieu de mémoire et d'histoire: Le Mémorial du martyr juif inconnu," in *Les Juifs entre la mémoire et l'oubli,* ed. Foulek Ringelheim (Brussels: Editions de l'Université de Bruxelles, 1987), 107–32.

79. YIVO was founded in Vilna in 1925 and played a key role in promoting the field of Jewish history. In 1940, a large part of its archives and its library were transferred to New York.

80. Letter of June 14, 1947, in *Shatski-bukh,* ed. Y. Lifshits (New York: YIVO, 1958), 193–94. Quoted in Robert Moses Shapiro, "Jacob Shatsky, Historian of Warsaw Jewry," *Polin: A Journal of Polish-Jewish Studies* 3 (1988): 209.

81. Jacob Shatzky, "Problemen fur yiddisher historiografye," in Lifshits, *Shatski-bukh,* 105–6. Quoted in Shapiro, "Jacob Shatsky," 209.

82. Joseph Tenenbaum, "Dr. Yankev Shatski–polihistor un histograf (an opshatsung)" in Lifshits, *Shatski-bukh,* 30–31. Quoted in Shapiro, "Jacob Shatsky," 209–10.

83. These developments in the life of Jacob Shatsky are charted in Shapiro, "Jacob Shatsky," 200–213.

84. Adolf Rudnicki, "The Clear Stream," in *The Dead and the Living Sea and Other Stories,* trans. Jadwiga Zwolska (Warsaw: Polonia Publishing House, 1957), 257–82, 258–59.

85. Quoted in Jarosław M. Rymkiewicz, *The Final Station: Umschlagplatz,* trans. Nina Taylor (New York: Farrar, Strauss, Giroux, 1994), 327.

II. The Advent of the Witness

1. To cite only a few examples: Tom Segev for Israel in *The Seventh Million;* Rochelle G. Saidel for the United States in *Never Too Late to Remember;* Annette Wieviorka for France, "Autour d'Auschwitz," in *Allemagne France: Lieux de mémoire d'une histoire commune,* ed. Jacques Moritz and Horst Müller (Paris: Albin Michel, 1995), 187–205.

2. Ben-Gurion, quoted in Segev, *The Seventh Million,* 326.

3. I return here to certain events already discussed in my *Procès Eichmann* (Brussels: Éditions Complexe, 1989). Ben-Gurion is quoted from a letter made public on May 27 and reproduced in *Le Monde* on May 28, 1960.

4. Abba Eban, *My Country: The Story of Modern Israel* (New York: Random House, 1972), 180–81.

5. Ibid., 181.

6. Françoise Ouzan, *Ces Juifs dont l'Amérique ne voulait pas: 1945–1950* (Bruxelles: Éditions Complexe, 1995). This is the only study published in French on the fate of Jewish survivors in displaced person camps in postwar Germany.

7. Adenauer's declaration is quoted in Segev, *The Seventh Million,* 202.

8. Serge Barcellini and Annette Wieviorka, *Passant, souviens-toi! Lieux du souvenir de la Seconde Guerre mondiale en France* (Paris: Plon, 1995).

9. Antoine Prost, *Les anciens combatants et la société française, 1914–1939* (Paris: Presses de la fondation des sciences politiques, 1997), vol. 1, *Histoire,* 132.

10. Ibid., 133.

11. Ibid., 136.

12. Dennis L. Bark and David R. Gress, *A History of West Germany,* vol. 1, *From Shadow to Substance 1945– 1963* (Oxford, U.K.: Basil Blackwell, 1989), 69.

13. Christopher Browning, *Ordinary Men: Reserve Police Battalion 101 and the Final Solution in Poland* (New York: Aaron Asher Books, 1992).

14. Segev, *The Seventh Million,* 324–26.

15. Gideon Hausner, *Justice in Jerusalem* (New York: Harper and Row, 1966), 292.

16. Annette Wieviorka, *Le procès de Nuremberg* (Rennes: Ouest-France-Mémorial, 1995).

17. Didier Lazard, *Le procès de Nuremberg: Récit d'un témoin* (Paris: Éditions de la Nouvelle Presse, 1947), 38.

18. Hausner, *Justice in Jerusalem,* 291.

19. Ibid., 292.

20. Geoffrey Hartman, "Learning from Survivors: The Yale Testimony Project," in *The Longest Shadow: In the Aftermath of the Holocaust* (Bloomington: Indiana University Press, 1996), 134.

21. Ibid., 138. I met Geoffrey Hartman in Paris in 1990. He entrusted me with the task of establishing the French satellite of the Fortunoff Archive. The organization "Té-

moignage pour mémoire" has thus collected some 130 testimonies deposited in the National Archives of France and available for consultation by students and researchers. Geoffrey Hartman and I have had long conversations on each of his visits to Paris. He confirmed to me that he had never read Gideon Hausner's book.

22. Hausner, *Justice in Jerusalem,* 293.

23. See above, chap. 1, 7.

24. Hausner, *Justice in Jerusalem,* 293–94.

25. Simone Veil, quoted in Wieviorka, *Déportation et génocide,* 170.

26. William Helmreich, *Against All Odds: Holocaust Survivors and the Successful Lives They Made in America* (New York: Simon & Schuster, 1992). Quoted in Alvin Rosenfeld, "The Americanization of the Holocaust," in *Thinking about the Holocaust: After Half a Century,* ed. Alvin H. Rosenfeld (Bloomington: Indiana University Press, 1997), 136. Bracketed addition is Rosenfeld's.

27. Segev, *The Seventh Million,* 185.

28. Hausner, *Justice in Jerusalem,* 295.

29. Ibid., 296.

30. Ibid.

31. "The Duty of Memory" (1983), interview with Anna Bravo and Federico Cereja, in *The Voice of Memory: Interviews 1961–1987,* by Primo Levi, ed. Marco Belpoliti and Robert Gordon, trans. Robert Gordon (Cambridge, U.K.: Polity Press, 2001), 223.

32. Louise Alcan, *Le temps écartelé* (Saint-Jean-de-Maurienne: Impr. Truchet 1980), 80.

33. Lawrence Douglas, *Memory of Judgment* (New Haven, Conn.: Yale University Press, 2001), 102.

34. *The Trial of Adolf Eichmann: Record of Proceedings in the District Court of Jerusalem,* 9 vols. (Jerusalem: Trust for the Publication of the Proceedings of the Eichmann Trial, in co-operation with the Israel State Archives and Yad Vashem, the Holocaust Martyrs' and Heroes' Remembrance Authority, 1992–), 1:208.

35. Haim Gouri, *Facing the Glass Booth: The Jerusalem Trial of Adolf Eichmann,* trans. Michael Swirsky (Detroit: Wayne State University Press, 2004), 28.

36. The trial proceedings are available in Hebrew, German, French, Yiddish [and English], and can be consulted at the Center for the Documentation of Contemporary Jewry. The French version is a transcript of the simultaneous translation made during the trial. I have relied on this text, improving the quality of the translation, which is often imprecise. Ada Lichtman testified during the twentieth session of the trial on April 28, 1961. TN: The translation is based on *The Trial of Adolf Eichmann,* the English version of the proceedings, modified where necessary to conform to the French. Lichtman's testimony is at 1:323–26.

37. *The Trial of Adolf Eichmann,* 1:324.

38. Ibid.

39. Ibid., 1:326.

40. The importance of this testimony had escaped me until I read Lawrence Douglas's book in manuscript, which called my attention to this witness, for which I thank him.

41. Douglas, *The Memory of Judgment,* 103. The commentator quoted is Natan Alterman.

42. Léon Poliakov, *Le procès de Jerusalem, jugements, documents* (Paris: Éditions du Centre, 1963), 44.

43. Leon Wells, *The Janowska Road* (New York: Macmillan, 1963); *Pour que la terre se souvienne,* translated from the English by Catherine and Jacques Legris (Paris: Albin Michel, 1962).

44. Gouri, *Facing the Glass Booth,* 38.

45. Georges Wellers, *De Drancy à Auschwitz* (Paris: Éditions du Centre, 1946).

46. Ka-tzetnik 135633, *House of Dolls* (New York: Simon and Schuster, 1955).

47. *The Trial of Adolf Eichmann,* 3:1237.

48. Ibid., 3:1237.

49. TN: The films of the Eichmann trial were recovered

and restored after the publication of this work. Some of the footage is included in the film *The Specialist* (communication with the author).

50. *The Trial of Adolf Eichmann,* 3:1198.

51. Lanzmann, *Shoah: The Complete Text,* 4.

52. Gouri, *Facing the Glass Booth,* 37.

53. Jean-Michel Frodon, "'L'expert': Film-enquête sur la visiblité du mal," *Le Monde,* September 24, 1997.

54. Segev, *The Seventh Million,* 350.

55. Gouri, *Facing the Glass Booth,* 20.

56. Ibid., 140.

57. Ibid.

58. Ibid., 269.

59. Ibid., 140.

60. Hannah Arendt, *Eichmann in Jerusalem: A Report on the Banality of Evil* (New York: Penguin, 1963), 224.

61. Ibid., 19.

62. Ibid., 20.

63. Annette Wieviorka, "'Solution finale' et *Hurbn:* Essai d'historiographie," in *Mille ans de cultures ashkénazes,* ed. Jean Baumgarten, Rachel Ertel, Itzhok Niborski, and Annette Wieviorka. A new historiography that reconciles these two perspectives, skillfully connecting microhistory to larger movements, is starting to emerge, as is demonstrated by Saul Friedländer's remarkable *Nazi Germany and the Jews,* vol. 1, *The Years of Persecution, 1933–1939* (New York: Harper-Collins, 1997).

64. Léon Poliakov, *L'envers du destin: Entretiens avec Georges Elia Sarfati* (Paris: Éditions de Fallois, 1989), 67.

65. Daniel Jonah Goldhagen, *Hitler's Willing Executioners* (New York: Knopf, 1996), 22.

66. Henri Raczymow, *Un cri sans voix* (Paris: Gallimard, 1985). Translated as *Writing the Book of Esther,* trans. Dori Katz (New York: Holmes & Meier, 1995).

67. Goldhagen, *Hitler's Willing Executioners,* 22.

68. Ibid., 24.

69. Arendt, *Eichmann in Jerusalem,* 19.

70. Marc Bloch, *The Historian's Craft,* trans. Peter Putnam (New York: Knopf, 1959), 140.

71. Raul Hilberg, "The Goldhagen Phenomenon," *Critical Inquiry* 23, no. 4 (Summer 1997): 721–28.

III. The Era of the Witness

1. Frédéric Gaussen, "Le goût pour les récits de vie," *Le Monde,* February 14, 1982.

2. Quoted in Ilan Avisar, *Screening the Holocaust: Cinema's Images of the Unimaginable* (Bloomington: Indiana University Press, 1988), 130.

3. Elie Wiesel reprints his review of *Holocaust* in the second volume of his memoirs, *And the Sea Is Never Full,* trans. Marion Wiesel (New York: Knopf, 1999), 117–22.

4. Quoted in Henry Rousso, *The Vichy Syndrome: History and Memory in France since 1944,* trans. Arthur Goldhammer (Cambridge, Mass.: Harvard University Press, 1991), 146.

5. Jacques Walter, "Dispositifs télévisuels et identités médiatiques des survivants. 'Vie et mort dans les camps Nazis,'" in *Cahier international sur le témoignage audiovisuel* (Brussels: Fondation Auschwitz, 1998), 164.

6. Hartman, "Learning from Survivors," 143.

7. Ibid., 136.

8. "Jewish Values in a Post-Holocaust Future: A Symposium," *Judaism* 16, no. 3 (Summer 1967): 269–99, 288, 291. Quoted in Jean-Michel Chaumont, *La concurrence des victimes: Génocide, identité, reconnaissance* (Paris: Éditions La Découverte, 1997), 113–14.

9. Leon Uris, foreword to *Promises to Keep,* by Ernst Michel (New York: Barricade Books, 1994), xiii. Quoted in Rosenfeld, "The Americanization of the Holocaust," 119–50, 137.

10. Raymond Aron, *De Gaulle, Israël et les Juifs* (Paris: Plon, 1968).

11. "Les Juifs de France ont-ils changé?" roundtable discussion, *Esprit* (April 1968): 581-82. Chaired by Jean-Marie Domenach, the roundtable included, in addition to Richard Marienstras, Pierre Vidal-Naquet, Wladimir Rabi, Paul Thibaud, and Alex Derczansky.

12. Ibid.

13. Jacques Walter, "Dispositifs télévisuels," 13.

14. Named after Alan Fortunoff, whose donation in 1987 made it possible to hire an archivist and to house the archive in the prestigious Sterling Memorial Library at Yale University.

15. On the state of the Fortunoff Archive, see the text by Joanne Rudof in *Ces visages qui nous parlent,* 67-70.

16. Hartman, "Learning from Survivors," 133.

17. Quoted in Annick Cojean, "Les voix de l'indicible," *Le Monde,* April 25, 1995. TN: Where possible, the translation draws on Laub's contributions to Shoshana Felman and Dori Laub, *Testimony: Crises in Witnessing in Literature, History, and Psychoanalysis* (New York: Routledge, 1991), 78, 142.

18. Steven Spielberg, in *Libération,* April 20, 1995.

19. Jacques Walter, "Les archives de l'histoire audiovisuelle des survivants de la Shoah," unpublished manuscript.

20. TN: In the early years of the project, Spielberg stated the goal of interviewing 150,000 witnesses by 2000 ("Recording Holocaust Testimony," *New York Times,* November 10, 1994). In 2001, after collecting 52,000 testimonies, the Spielberg Foundation declared that it had "completed its mission of videotaping 50,000 eyewitnesses to the Holocaust" and discontinued the interviewing of survivors ("Shoah Foundation Sets New International Education Mission, Expands Efforts to Overcome Prejudice, Intolerance, and Bigotry," press release dated August 17, 2001. Downloaded 2/5/05 from http://www.vfh.org).

21. www.vhf.org.

22. *Libération,* January 12, 1998.

23. Wieviorka and Niborski, *Les livres du souvenir,* 172.

24. Fifty dollars per interview.

25. *Libération,* January 12, 1998.

26. Ibid.

27. This was the title chosen by Alvin H. Rosenfeld for his contribution to *Thinking about the Holocaust.*

28. Rosenfeld, "The Americanization of the Holocaust," 123.

29. Avisar, *Screening the Holocaust,* 96–97. Quoted in Rosenfeld, "The Americanization of the Holocaust," 124.

30. Philippe Lejeune, ed., *"Cher Cahier . . .": Témoignages sur le journal personnel* (Paris: Gallimard "Témoins," 1989).

31. Bruno Bettelheim, *Surviving and Other Essays* (New York: Knopf, 1979), 247.

32. Ibid., 250.

33. Ibid., 251.

34. Quoted in Rosenfeld, "The Americanization of the Holocaust," 126.

35. Undated, four-page letter of solicitation by Miles Lerman, chairman, United States Holocaust Memorial Museum. Quoted in Rosenfeld, "The Americanization of the Holocaust," 127.

36. Michael Berenbaum, *After Tragedy and Triumph: Essays in Modern Jewish Thought and Experience* (Cambridge, U.K.: Cambridge University Press, 1990), 20. Quoted in Rosenfeld, "The Americanization of the Holocaust," 129–30.

37. Roberta Smith, "Holocaust Museum Adjusting to Relentless Flood of Visitors," *New York Times,* December 23, 1993. Correction January 11, 1994. Quoted without correction in Rosenfeld, "The Americanization of the Holocaust," 130.

38. Quoted in Federico Cereja, "Contre l'oubli," in *Le Devoir de mémoire: Entretien avec Anna Bravo et Feder-*

ico Cereja, by Primo Levi (Paris: Mille et une Nuits, 1995), 74.

39. Anna-Lise Stern, "Sois déportée . . . et témoigne! Psychanalyser, témoigner: Doublebind," in *La Shoah: Témoignages, savoirs, oeuvres,* ed. Annette Wieviorka and Claude Mouchard (Saint-Denis: Presses Universitaires de Vincennes, 1999), 17.

40. Henri Borlant, "Passe-moi le sel," in *La Shoah: Témoignages, savoirs, oeuvres.*

41. Robert Antelme, "Poetry and Testimony of the Camps, Followed by Two Poems by Maurice Honel," in *On Robert Antelme's The Human Race: Essays and Commentary,* ed. Daniel Dobbels, trans. Jeffrey Haight (Evanston, Ill.: Marlboro Press, 2003), 31. Antelme's essay was originally published in *Le patriote résistant* no. 23 (May 15, 1948).

42. Beyrak, "To Rescue the Individual," 137.

43. Stern, "Sois déportée," 16.

44. Quoted in Stern, "Sois déportée," 16.

45. Philippe Lejeune, *Pour l'autobiographie: Chroniques* (Paris: Seuil, 1998), 28.

46. Ibid., 48.

47. Pierre Laborie, "Histoire et résistance: Des historiens trouble-mémoire," in *Écrire l'histoire du temps present: En hommage à François Bédarida* (Paris: CNRS, 1993), 140–41.

48. Marcel Lévy, *La vie et moi* (Paris: Phoebus Libretto, 1998), 43.

49. TN: http://www.vhf.org, June 11, 1998. Accessible via web.archive.org. (<http://web.archive.org/web/19980611075500/http://www.vhf.org/>)

50. "The Duty of Memory," 231–32.

51. Stern, "Sois déportée," 22.

52. Beyrak, "To Rescue the Individual," 100.

53. See Wieviorka, *Déportation et génocide.*

54. Ruth Klüger, *Still Alive: A Holocaust Girlhood Remembered* (New York: Feminist Press of the City University of New York, 2001), 112.

55. Quoted in Beyrak, "To Rescue the Individual," 137.

56. Hausner, *Justice in Jerusalem*, 323–24.

57. Dominique Mehl, *La télévision de l'intimité* (Paris: Seuil, 1996), 11–12.

58. Ibid., 13.

59. Ibid., 28.

60. Richard Sennett, *The Fall of Public Man* (New York: Vintage Books, 1974), 259. Quoted in Mehl, *La télévision,* 154.

61. Philippe Lejeune, *The Autobiographical Pact,* ed. Paul John Eakin, trans. Katherine Leary (Minneapolis: University of Minnesota Press, 1989).

62. Mehl, *La télévision,* 212.

Epilogue

1. Éric Conan, *Le procès Papon: Un journal d'audience* (Paris: Gallimard, 1998), 102.

2. Pascale Nivelle, in *Crimes contre l'humanité: Barbie, Touvier, Bousquet, et Papon,* by Sorj Challandon and Pascale Nivelle, (Paris: Plon, 1998), 409.

3. Bertrand Poirot-Delpech, *Papon: Un crime de bureau* (Paris: Stock, 1998), 116.

4. Conan, *Le procès Papon,* 104–5.

5. Berthe Burko-Falcman, *L'enfant caché* (Paris: Seuil, 1997).